CURIOUS CATS AND FANTASTICAL FELINES

Dedicated to Hector and Jayfeather.
And to cat-lovers everywhere.

First published in the United Kingdom
in 2026 by
Batsford
43 Great Ormond Street
London
WC1N 3HZ

An imprint of B. T. Batsford Holdings Limited

ISBN 9781849949736

A CIP catalogue record for this book is available from the British Library.

10 9 8 7 6 5 4 3 2 1

Reproduction by Rival Colour Ltd., UK
Printed by Dream Colour, China

This book can be ordered direct from the publisher at
www.batsfordbooks.com, or try your local bookshop.

Distributed throughout the UK and Europe by Abrams & Chronicle Books,
1st Floor, 22–24 Ely Place, London EC1N 6TE and 57 rue Gaston Tessier,
75166 Paris, France

www.abramsandchronicle.co.uk
info@abramsandchronicle.co.uk

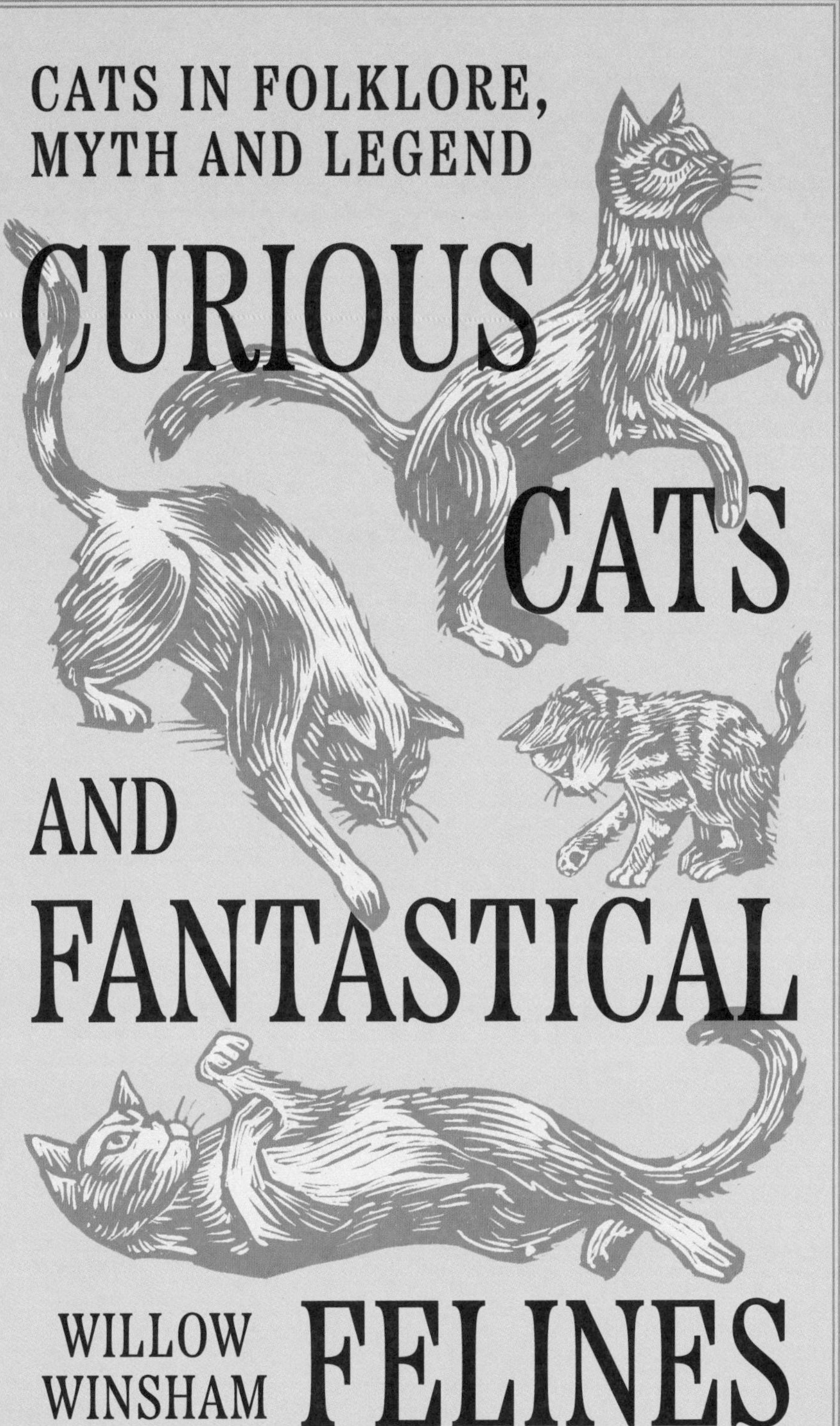

CATS IN FOLKLORE, MYTH AND LEGEND

CURIOUS CATS AND FANTASTICAL FELINES

WILLOW WINSHAM

BATSFORD

Contents

PART 2:
Cats of Fairy Tale, Lore and Legend 94

Introduction

The complex, intertwined history of cats and humankind is believed to stretch back at least ten thousand years.

When peripatetic hunter-gathering societies gradually shifted towards arable farming and more permanent settlements, one of the many advantages was the ability to store food for longer and in greater quantities than before. Such a change presented fresh challenges, however, one of which – vermin – could mean the difference between life and death, particularly during the harsh months of winter.

Mice and rats thrived where grain and other crops were stored, but help was at hand. Cats, drawn by a plentiful supply of food, inadvertently aided humans by ridding them of these pests; in turn, grateful farmers provided board and lodging for their feline saviours, and an alliance based on mutual interest was born. The cat, which even then knew when it was onto a good thing, has maintained this relationship ever since.

It is generally believed that domestication of the cat – *Felis catus* – first occurred in the Fertile Crescent, an area encompassing parts of West Asia such as Kuwait, Iraq, Iran, Syria, Jordan, Israel, Lebanon and Egypt – the very area in which humankind itself is believed to have originated. From here the cat soon spread – through trade, human movement and natural roaming – and today, Antarctica is the only continent in the world to not have a domestic cat presence of some kind.

Throughout this long and chequered history, cats have been revered as deities, persecuted as witches and demons, and are the subject of countless myths and legends, superstitions and beliefs. Cats are one of the most popular pets worldwide, coming second only to the faithful dog, and whether a cat lover or hater, it is rare to find someone entirely indifferent to their presence. Indeed, they are so beloved by humankind that there is even a word for a love or great fondness of cats: ailurophilia.

This book is an exploration of the varied and often strange ways in which cats are represented within folklore across the globe. The aim is both to celebrate these marvellous creatures, and also to bring us to a closer understanding not only of cats, but also of humankind as a whole and the world that we share with our feline companions.

Note: It is important to note that, throughout history, there have been many beliefs that have led to cruel and brutal treatment of cats and animals in general. While some mention of such practices is unavoidable, they are not the focus of this book and references to animal cruelty will be kept to a minimum.

PART

Sayings, Superstitions and Strange Beliefs

One of the easiest ways to identify what a culture or society considers important is to look at the focus of the sayings and superstitions prevalent in any given time or area. Through these we glimpse humankind's greatest hopes and most deep-rooted fears: what we love, what we hate, and what we regard as our most deadly threats, both real and imagined.

Cats, unsurprisingly given their prominence in our lives, feature heavily in superstitions and sayings across the globe, with a variety of outcomes – both good and bad – being attributed to them and their behaviours. Whether crossing the road or washing their paws in front of the fire, no movement or behaviour is considered too insignificant where the cat is concerned: every twitch of their tail imbued with the greatest significance.

So, what do the actions of our faithful felines say about them, and, perhaps more importantly, about us?

Fateful Felines: Good and Bad Fortune

Due to the often unpredictable and harsh realities of existence, humankind has long been preoccupied with what the future may hold, and for thousands of years people the world over have scrutinized their environments for each and every sign that luck – good or bad – might be coming their way.

Perhaps to a greater extent than any other single animal, cats have become linked in our collective consciousness with ideas surrounding luck, and, over time, have garnered a reputation for not only being able to predict, but also to influence, our fates.

Unlucky for Some: Black Cats

More than any other colour, black cats feature prominently in feline-related folklore. While it is generally agreed that black cats can influence a person's fortune, opinion is divided as to whether they are a force for good or bad.

Despite the generally negative connotations of more recent times, black cats were traditionally considered lucky in the United Kingdom. Several sources attest to the belief that a black cat would keep trouble away from a household, and that if one came to a house it was a good idea to welcome it – and the good fortune it promised – inside. If the cat was later lost, however, bad luck and sorrow would soon follow.

Due to the strong belief in their fortune-bringing properties, black cats were such a treasured commodity in Scarborough, Yorkshire, that they were often stolen, as sailors' wives firmly believed that such creatures would keep their husbands safe while away at sea.

It is also said that black cats can prove to be lucky where love is concerned: an English saying states that, 'Wherever the cat of the house is black. The lasses o' lovers will have no lack.' A belief recorded in Cornwall suggests that it was lucky to see a black cat when on the way to church to be married, but opinion seems to be divided on this, as in Somerset there was a contrary belief that it was unlucky to meet a cat – of any colour – on your wedding day.

The ill-fated English monarch, King Charles I, is said to have had a black cat that he favoured most highly. His thoughts on black cats can be gleaned from the name he gave this pet: Luck. According to legend, Charles believed that whatever happened to the treasured feline would be reflected in the fate of the nation. This might well have proven true, as it was said that Luck disappeared or died the day before the king was arrested.

In some areas of France, black cats were linked to the discovery of hidden treasure. It was said that taking a cat to the intersection of five roads, setting it down and following where it led would result in uncovering great riches.

Across the Atlantic in the USA, opinion is again divided when it comes to black cats. In La Harpe, Illinois, in the early 20th century, it was the circumstances rather than the black cat itself that decided your fortune. While it was bad luck for a black cat to run across someone's path, it was good luck for one to come to your house. Another generally held belief was that, while it was unlucky to give a black cat away, lending it to someone would bring good luck to the owner. In some areas, however, the reputation of black cats was less positive: in Georgia, a completely black cat was said to be a witch, and rubbing its fur at night would reveal the fire it had brought with it from hell.

One very popular belief regarding black cats is that it is highly unlucky for one to cross your path. This is a prevalent belief in many areas of the world, including the USA and several parts of Europe.

Sometimes the direction in which the cat is travelling is important. In Germany, if a cat crosses from right to left, then this is considered bad luck, but if it crosses left to right then it is seen as a good sign instead. In Japan, a black cat crossing your path is regarded as a good omen.

The time of day that a black cat sighting takes place can have an impact: a belief stemming from at least the 17th century suggested it was particularly bad luck to meet a black cat early in the morning. Sometimes the number of cats seen also plays a part: in India, seeing three black cats together is said to be a sign of good luck.

As with many superstitions regarding bad luck, there are ways in which the misfortune of a black cat crossing your path can be counteracted. In the UK and other areas, spitting after seeing a cat was said to be an antidote, while in Norway and Sweden, spitting three times was believed to do the trick. According to Southern Appalachian folklore in the USA, the bad luck can be negated by spitting quickly on the cat's tracks after it has crossed in front of you.

In Turkey, black cats are considered to bring bad fortune. If you see a black cat it is advisable to touch your hair or something black to counteract the bad luck that may befall you, and people will change their path to avoid these sadly maligned creatures.

Conversely, it is *white* cats that have historically been considered unlucky across many areas of the UK. In Wales, there was said to be one exception to this rule: if a pure white cat was kept with a pure black one, then the bad luck would be cancelled out and the household would experience good fortune. Folklorist and writer Katharine Briggs likewise related an anecdote from the Cotswolds area of England where her neighbour had a pure white cat: she was advised to quickly get a black one to counteract the bad luck the white would bring on its own.

Where does the idea of black cats being unlucky come from? It is generally accepted that the cat's perceived links with witchcraft and evil magic have at least in part been responsible for this unfortunate and long-held association. While the original link may have been long forgotten, the prejudice against black cats continues today, and black cats and dogs are less likely to be adopted from animal shelters than those of other colours.

In an attempt to counteract the bad press black felines have accrued, both the UK and USA have special days to raise their profile: Black Cat Appreciation day in the United States is 17 August, while in the UK it is 27 October. The aim of both days is to raise awareness of, and to celebrate, the positives of black cat ownership, and to hopefully go some way to redress the balance in their favour.

But what of cats in general when it comes to luck? Again, opinion has been greatly divided. In Ireland, cats have been long been considered with suspicion: a common response when entering a house was some variant of: 'God save all, barring the cat!'

Cats are generally considered lucky in the theatre, but only if they stay safely behind the scenes: if a cat walks across the stage while a performance is in progress, this is said to be very bad luck. It is also considered bad luck for an actor to kick a cat, and it is said that they should be treated with respect.

A strong taboo existed against cats among the mining communities of Cornwall, UK; saying the word 'cat' or talking about them in any way while underground was highly frowned upon. Moreover, if a cat somehow strayed into the mines, miners would refuse point blank to work on the level where it had been spotted until the cat was removed. In Ayrshire, south-west Scotland, it was said that if a miner encountered a cat – in particular a black one – on the way to the mine, then he would turn around and go home again, taking it as a sign of misfortune ahead.

It was not only black cats that were thought to influence our love lives. It was said that if a cat sneezed once near a bride on the morning of her wedding, then the marriage would be happy and prosperous. In general, if a cat chose to live in a household, this was good news for any unmarried daughters there, as it meant that marriage was on the cards in the future.

What did it mean to dream of a cat? In a collection of dream interpretations from ancient Egypt, dating from c. 1980–1801 BCE, it was stated that if a man dreamed of seeing a large cat it was a good omen, meaning he would have a large harvest.

The Curse of the May Kitten

According to folklore in many parts of England and Wales, you should take note of the month in which your kitten or cat was born: if they happened to be born in May, you might be in for a bumpy ride indeed. Welsh lore states that cats born in this month were prone to bring snakes into a house, a belief also recorded in Dorset and elsewhere. Although not always a reliable narrator, folklorist Ruth Tongue echoed a similar sentiment from Somerset, relating how cats born in May would catch no mice and would instead litter the house with toads and spiders, and it is likely that such beliefs were widespread.

Kittens born in October just after Michaelmas (29 September, or 11 October according to the old calendar) were also known for mischief and bad behaviour. Such kittens were known as 'berry kits' due to this time coinciding with the end of the blackberry season, their wild behaviour attributed to the connection with the Devil, whose fall to Earth was said to have been broken by a blackberry bush.

Puss in Boots: Constantino and His Cat

Once upon a time there lived in Bohemia a woman named Soriana. Soriana was very poor indeed, and owned only three things of any value: a kneading trough, a pastry board and a cat. Her life was not an easy one, and, with age and illness taking their toll, she made her will, leaving her belongings to her three sons. The oldest, Dusolino, was bequeathed the trough, the board was to go to the middle son Tesifone, and the cat to the youngest, Constantino Fortunato.

When Soriana was no longer in this world, the three brothers had to learn to make their own livings. The two older sons resourcefully lent out the trough and board to neighbours, and found themselves rewarded with cake and bread in return. They did not share such bounties with their younger brother, however, laughingly telling him to go and ask his cat instead.

Impoverished and unhappy, poor Constantino and his cat suffered greatly. But, fortunately for Constantino, it transpired that his was no ordinary cat: it was in fact a fairy in disguise. Seeing how his master was mistreated by his selfish siblings and taking umbrage on his behalf, the cat decided to take matters into his own paws. Much to Constantino's surprise, the cat spoke to him, telling him that he, the cat, would see Constantino looked after forthwith.

With that, the cat left his stunned master behind and went out into the fields. There he lay, pretending to be asleep, until a leveret, fooled by his ruse, rashly strayed too close. In a flash, the cat was upon it, killing the creature dead. Carrying his prize, the cat took it to the nearby palace, begging an audience with the king himself.

Curious at such a request, the king had the cat brought before him, and asked what he wanted. The cat duly told the king that his master, Constantino, had sent the leveret to the king as a gift. When the king, accepting the offering, enquired as to the identity of Constantino, the wily feline informed the king that his master was a man of the greatest good looks, and, more importantly, the highest virtue of any man ever known. Greatly impressed, the king set before the cat a great feast of meat and drink: the cat ate his fill before bagging up the plentiful remains and taking them home to the waiting Constantino. Constantino gratefully received this bounty and ate until he was full. When his brothers, saw the abundant feast, they asked for a share but Constantino refused, repaying their bad treatment of him with the same in return.

Although the cat had, for now, solved the food situation, the beleaguered Constantino suffered from another affliction that caused him no small embarrassment. Despite his good looks, due to the harshness of his life thus far, the skin of his face and body was rough and sore, causing him great discomfort. How poor Constantino longed for relief! With this too the cat proved of great help: he took his master down to the river and licked him all over, leaving no patch of skin untouched. Under his cat's careful care, within days, Constantino's skin troubled him no more.

In the meantime, due to the success of the first attempt, the cat had continued to take gifts to the palace for the king. In this way, it was not long before the cat was providing enough for Constantino to live on and more besides, eventually raising his master from

poverty to relative comfort. The cat, however, started to grow weary of constantly travelling back and forth, and decided that the situation could be further improved upon. With this in mind, he told Constantino that he had another plan, and that, if he did as the cat bid him, he would be a rich man. Constantino wondered how this could possibly be achieved, but the cat simply told him to come with him and not worry about a thing, as his plan could not fail.

Constantino agreed, and the cat took him to a place on the river bank close to the palace. Once there, the cat told Constantino to remove his clothes and throw himself into the river. When Constantino had done as he directed, the cat started to call for help as loudly as he could, shouting that his master Constantino was drowning.

The king himself heard the cat's cries, and sent his men to help the one who had sent him so many gifts. Constantino was rescued from the water, dressed in dry clothes by the king's men and escorted to the king, who welcomed him warmly. But how, the king asked, had he come to be in the water in the first place? The cat again leapt to the rescue, informing the king that his master had been beset by a gang of robbers, with the aim of stealing the jewels he had been bringing to the king as a gift. They had taken the treasure, and then cast Constantino into the river. Aghast, the king immediately ordered that Constantino should be treated as a greatly honoured guest, with nothing spared for his comfort.

Noting his good looks and thinking him to be a man of great fortune, the king quickly decided that Constantino would make a very suitable husband for his daughter, Elisetta. The young woman, very much in agreement, brought with her gold and jewels and fine clothing as her dowry, and the marriage was celebrated across the land to great rejoicing from all.

After the festivities finally came to an end, a great procession formed to convey the newlyweds to their new home. Ten mules loaded with gold and five with fine garments set off, along with the bride and her retinue. Of course, Constantino was decidedly lacking in a suitable residence to receive his new wife, but the cat was quick to put him at ease, telling him again that he would manage everything.

The cat rode on ahead of the procession, soon leaving the others behind. Before long, he came across a band of knights, warning them that they would soon be attacked by a large group of armed men heading their way. The knights were rightly fearful, as they could hear the sound of the horses in the distance, and asked the cat what they should do. They need not worry said the cat: all they had to do was say that they were the men of Messer Constantino and they would be left alone. Greatly relieved, the knights agreed, and the cat continued on his way.

Next, the cat came across flocks of sheep and herds of cattle. He told the people tending them the same thing he had told the knights, again filling them with great fear. It would all be well, the cat consoled them, as long as they told the approaching men that the sheep and cattle belonged to Messer Constantino. And so it continued: every time the cat came upon a new group, he instructed them in the same way.

The plan worked perfectly: as the procession carrying the princess came across each group in turn, and her soldiers asked who the sheep or cows or fields belonged to, each replied that they belonged to Messer Constantino. Trusting in his cat, Constantino himself played his part in maintaining the ruse, nodding in assent every time he was asked if the land or men belonged to him.

He was still, however, without an abode worthy of his new-found status, and he was running out of time to remedy this fact. The cat, however – as with everything that had come before – had the matter well in hand. Still ahead of his master, the cat reached a castle. Although a fair size and in good repair, it was guarded by decidedly weak forces, a fact that could be used to his master's advantage. The cat wasted no time in informing the garrison that great ruin was fast approaching, as a force of soldiers was heading their way to butcher them all. They were greatly afraid but the cat, of course, provided the solution: tell them that the castle belonged to Messer Constantino Fortunato.

As everyone had done before, the soldiers did as they were bidden. When the procession arrived a short while later it was greeted with the information that the castle belonged to none other than Constantino himself, and the princess and her entourage entered the castle with great cheer. As luck would further have it (for Constantino at least), the actual owner of the castle had met with an unfortunate accident while travelling overseas, and would not be returning to dispute ownership. Constantino's ruse, therefore, was never discovered, and he and his wife made the castle their home.

Constantino's good fortune did not end there. When the king died, the people pronounced Constantino himself as their new ruler, thanks to his marriage to the old king's daughter. The couple lived a long, happy life, and their children were heirs to the kingdom Constantino had been granted, all thanks to the auspices of his faithful and clever cat.

Throwing a Black Cat: The Treasure of the Carbunclo

According to lore from Chiloé, Chile, the legendary *carbunclo* – a small, secretive animal with a glowing, coal-like stone on its head, said to have been first discovered by the 16th-century Spanish conquistadors – was a source of great luck and riches.

In one version of the story, a black cat is instrumental in locating and possessing this greatly coveted treasure. The treasure hunter, sporting a new shovel, must go at midnight to the place where the creature was last spotted. He should not go alone, however, but must take with him an old widow, who in turn is holding a black cat. As he digs he should keep track of how far down he goes, stopping once he reaches a depth of one rod – 5m (16.5ft).

The cat should then be thrown into the hole, where it will vanish, but the hunter should not be disheartened; as he continues to dig, the cat will appear once more, ready to be thrown again when another rod is reached. The process is to be repeated until the treasure is reached and the lucky treasure hunter finds his fortune.

However, there are great risks to the process. If the treasure hunter, in his haste to reach his riches, forgets to throw the cat at each rod, all will be lost. He will experience a terrible death in the hole he has dug, poisoned by the fumes given off by the very treasure he was seeking.

Japan's Inviting Cat: Maneki Neko

There was once a temple at Gotoku-ji, Tokyo. It was a small temple, so small that most did not even know of its existence, but it was there that the legend of the Maneki Neko was born.

Long ago there lived at the temple a monk who had a soft spot for a cat that frequented the area. Despite it being against the rules, the monk fed and nurtured the animal, continuing to do so even when he was told by the abbot himself to stop, and the two formed a firm friendship.

One fateful night, the powerful Lord Li Naotaka passed through the area: he was mid-journey when a terrible storm broke out. Rain lashed down, winds raging so wildly that he had no choice but to break his journey and take refuge from the elements. Sheltering with his men under a tree that provided scant protection, he intended to wait the storm out, quite unaware in the dark that a temple lay so close by.

Suddenly, Lord Li Naotaka saw something in the distance. It was a cat, but not like any cat he had ever seen before. This creature was sitting on its hind legs and appeared to be beckoning, gesturing for him to come towards it. Greatly intrigued, Li Naotaka followed: and not a moment too soon. For as he reached the safety of the Gotoku-ji temple, lightning struck the tree he had been sheltering under only moments before.

There was no doubt that the cat had saved him from certain death. Overwhelmed with gratitude towards the creature that had saved his life, Li Naotaka bestowed great riches on the temple, and it rose from obscurity to become a place of great renown. The temple at Gotoku-ji still thrives today: all because, it is said, of this feline saviour.

Fittingly, the cat became the temple's symbol, and today visitors can witness for themselves the thousands of beckoning cat figures – Maneki Neko – that decorate the temple in homage to this tale.

Thus goes one of the many variations of the origin story of the ubiquitous beckoning cat. Many places claim to be the birthplace of this iconic figure, and all have stories with a similar central theme: a beckoning cat gestures to someone and saves them from harm, and the person then goes on to make a figure of the cat in gratitude. This act in turn brings good fortune, both to the creator and those who own such a figure.

Another popular version of how the Maneki Neko came to be such a prominent symbol comes from Imado, Tokyo, dating from the early 19th century. In this tale, there lived a very poor old woman who eventually had to make the heartbreaking decision to sell her beloved cat. With a heavy heart she did so, only to dream the next night that the cat was speaking to her. Far from being angry with her for letting it go, the cat told the woman to make an image of it in clay. She did as instructed, and became wealthy from selling her figures at the Imado Shrine. These basic first incarnations were made of Imado-yaki pottery and were known as *marushime-neko*.

Today, the white porcelain cat with a bell round its neck, holding a coin and waving its hand to us, is a familiar sight across Japan and beyond. A common location for the Maneki

Neko is at the entrance to a shop or restaurant, beckoning in customers, and with them, it is hoped, luck and prosperity for the business will follow.

The Maneki Neko appears to have originated in the Edo period (1603–1868 CE). Although originally white, nowadays, Maneki Neko can be found in a wide array of colours, each representing luck in one of many areas of life. Generally, gold Maneki Neko are said to bring financial prosperity and red is for successful relationships; while a black Maneki Neko offers protection from evil spirits. If you are looking for good health, a green Maneki Neko is your best bet, whereas pink will be beneficial to your love life. Academic success is said to be guaranteed by a blue Maneki Neko.

Great significance is likewise placed on which hand the Maneki Neko has raised. Details vary from location to location, and even person to person, and there are many different ideas as to what each hand means. For some, the left hand represents business, while the right stands for home. The left hand raised is beckoning in money, while if the right hand is lifted, it is bringing in the customers. If you can't decide which is more important, then the Maneki Neko with two hands beckoning is the one for you. The height of the paw is also said to influence how much benefit the cat will bring: the higher the paw, the greater the luck.

Matters of Life and Death

Understandably, humankind has long been fascinated by matters of life and death. This has developed into both a healthy watchfulness for perceived danger and, furthermore, a heightened interest in perceived signs or omens regarding whether our days are numbered.

Cats have been linked to ideas of life and death, and good or ill health, in a variety of ways. Whether intentional or not, through their own actions or as unwilling participants, cats have been credited with an uncanny ability to influence our existence.

The Nine Lives of a Cat

Among the various popular beliefs surrounding cats is the idea that they are gifted with not one but nine lives. Unfortunately for cat lovers everywhere, cats of course don't really die and then come back again another eight times. But, as anyone who shares their lives with a feisty feline can attest, it can certainly seem at times that they live charmed lives, emerging unscathed from a variety of scrapes and predicaments. Where then does this familiar belief come from?

The origin of the idea that a cat has nine lives is believed to be an Old English proverb: 'A cat has nine lives. For three he plays, for three he strays, and for the last three he stays.' It is hard to say exactly when this first appeared, but the idea of the nine-lived cat was already established by the late 16th century, with Shakespeare referencing the saying in *Romeo and Juliet* when Mercutio says to Tybalt, 'Good King of cats, nothing but one of your nine lives.' The phrase isn't explained in the text, heavily suggesting that it was a common enough concept without further detail being necessary.

But what does it actually mean? One suggested explanation is that the saying refers to the different stages of a cat's life: first as a kitten, then a roaming cat, and then finally as an elderly cat enjoying the rest of its days resting by the fire.

There is also a supposed link between the nine lives of a cat and witches. A proverb recorded in 1546 states that, 'No wife, a woman hath nine lives like a cat.' This idea was further elaborated on later in the same century in William Baldwin's satirical novel, *Beware the Cat* (1561): 'A Cat hath nine lives, that is to say, a witch may take on her a cat's body nine times.' In 1788, in *A Classical Dictionary of the Vulgar Tongue*, Francis Grose recorded the belief that cats have nine lives, one less than women, again indicating that this idea was commonly known.

Why nine lives? The number nine is considered a special or significant number in several cultures and religions, including Hinduism, Christianity, Chinese culture and Norse mythology. It is often seen as particularly important as it is the product of three times three – which in itself is a number imbued with great significance and power.

Although nine is the most common number of lives ascribed to cats, there are, however, variations. In Italy, Spain, Greece and Brazil, cats are said to have seven lives each, and in some Arabic speaking areas including Turkey, a cat has to make do with just six.

Today, cats having nine lives remains a common idea in popular culture. Among other numerous examples, it is a central theme in the highly popular *Warrior Cats* book series by Erin Hunter: each new clan leader is granted nine lives by the ancestor cats of Star Clan as a mark of their approval.

Take Your Breath Away

Even today, the idea that a cat shouldn't be left alone with a baby is something still told to parents – especially first-time ones – and there are various guards and nets available to purchase with the express purpose of keeping the family cat out of the baby's cot or pram.

What many people likely don't realize is how this idea originated: an old belief that cats are capable of stealing a person's breath. It is unclear how far this idea goes back, but the belief that the breath and saliva of cats was capable of destroying the lungs was recorded in an early 17th-century source that states it was a bad idea to have a cat in bed as the air would be corrupted and the individual would fall into 'fever … and consumptions'.

An often-cited incident used to support the breath-sucking tendencies of cats was reported in the *Annual Register* for 1791. An entry for 25 January of that year recorded that near the city of Plymouth in south-west England, an 18-month-old child was discovered dead. The coroner investigating the case ruled that the child had died 'in consequence of a cat sucking its breath', which had led in turn to 'a strangulation'.

In Somerset during the 18th century and onwards, it was believed that a cat in or on the bed would suck the breath of the person sleeping there. Cats born in May – generally understood to be unlucky – were said to be particularly inclined to do this. In some areas, it was said that a baby sleeping with a cat would end up sucking in cat hairs and then choke or suffocate on them. Some even believed that a cat could not only suck out your air, but, according to a 19th-century supplement to the Jamieson's *Dictionary of Scots*, they could suck a person's blood as well.

Over time, the idea that a cat could suck the breath from an individual evolved to include the idea that a cat would physically smother a sleeping child by lying upon it, a belief that is recorded from at least the 18th century and remains today.

There have been various explanations for this supposed behaviour. One popular idea was that cats are lured by the smell of milk on a baby: the cat, tempted by the milky smell, would smother the infant while trying to get to the milk. More recent theories, dating from the 20th century, include the idea that the cat is drawn to the warmth of the sleeping baby or, more sinisterly, that the cat is jealous of the human child that has displaced the cat in its owners' affections and is therefore actively removing its rival.

Of course it is possible that a cat could accidentally, tragically, smother a child if sleeping with it unattended. There is, however, no verifiable evidence that a cat would do this intentionally, or that it will suck the breath from a baby or other human being, while asleep or otherwise.

According to general superstition, it was said to be a bad idea even to raise a baby with a cat. This was even more of a problem if both cat and child happened to be born on the same day. It was believed that the child wouldn't thrive – the idea being that the cat would somehow take the life force for itself and not leave any for the baby, and as a consequence the cat would live and the child would die. In the UK as late as 1900 in Devon, it was believed bad luck to have both cat and baby in the house, and that the cat should be sent away to ensure the health of the human child.

The connection between cats and ill-effects on infants could extend to even before birth. In the 1980s, a woman from London related how her baby had been stillborn, giving the explanation that while she was pregnant, a cat 'went over me'.

Kill or Cure

The influence of cats upon our health was not always negative, and, according to folk belief, cats could also be instrumental in providing relief from a variety of ailments.

Black cats were said to be particularly effective against eye complaints. According to an 18th-century belief, rubbing the tail of a black cat across a stye on the eyelid was believed to bring relief to the sufferer. A variation from the mid-19th century had to be carried out on the first night of a new moon: the afflicted was to pull one single hair from the tail of a black cat before rubbing the tail tip over the stye nine – or in some cases, seven – times.

A suggested remedy for whooping cough was to finely chop nine hairs from a black cat's tail and bake them in water. This was then ingested by the sufferer to effect the desired cure.

The belief that illness could be transferred from the sufferer to an animal was common: according to *The County Housewife's Family Companion* of 1750, a woman with a swollen hand had achieved relief by inserting her finger into the ear of the household cat. Within two hours she was pain free – to the detriment of the cat however, which was said to have suffered terribly. According to a 20th-century belief in Somerset, all a cat had to do was lick an afflicted area of the body and it would be cured.

From *Titanic* to *Lusitania*: Cats and Shipwrecks

Animals are often credited with possessing a sixth sense; an uncanny knack for knowing something bad is about to occur before it is perceptible to humans. Like the proverbial rats deserting a sinking ship, there are several legends relating to cats having a similar skill, with such feline foreshadowing said to have taken place before some of the greatest seaborne disasters of the 20th century.

Doubtless the most famous shipwreck in history is that of the British ocean liner RMS *Titanic*. On the night of 15 April 1912, *Titanic* struck an iceberg; the ship broke apart and sank to the bottom of the North Atlantic Ocean, causing the deaths of over 1,500 passengers and crew from the 2,200 on board.

The disaster has fascinated historians and the general public alike ever since, and countless words have been written about the sinking and the individuals who lost their lives on that fateful night. A fact perhaps not as well known is that there were also several animals on board: at least 12 dogs – three of which made it to safety in the lifeboats – and a variety of birds, including chickens, cockerels and at least one canary. There were also said to have been several cats on board, and one in particular, known as Jenny, has passed down into legend.

According to the general story, Jenny was ship's cat on board *Titanic*. She made her home in the galley kitchen, and was particularly friendly with a kitchen hand by the name of Jim. Jim and Jenny were the best of (ship)mates, and Jenny gave Jim the honour of allowing him to stroke her newborn kittens after they were born in her cosy nest. By all accounts, Jenny was calm and content, a willing passenger, used to life at sea.

The day before *Titanic* was set to sail from Southampton, however, Jenny decided to literally jump ship. Gathering up her kittens, she carried them, one by one, from their warm bed, dumping them onto the quayside. When she had the last one safe, she joined them, leaving behind her home and her friend.

Now, Jim, witnessing this desertion, was overcome with a sense of foreboding. If Jenny, a sensible, intuitive cat, had decided to leave, then perhaps she knew something that the rest of the crew didn't. Taking no chances, Jim decided that his time with *Titanic* had likewise come to an end, and the ship set sail without him.

And so it was that Jenny the ship's cat saved his life.

Although this might all sound rather fanciful, parts of the tale of Jenny and Jim at least can be substantiated as fact. The presence of a ship's cat aboard *Titanic* has been corroborated by two people: stewardess Violet Jessop, and Joseph 'Jim' Mulholland himself.

According to Jessop, who was 24 at the time of the tragedy, Jenny made herself at home in a cosy corner of the galley. She had been with the ship since leaving Belfast, and had given birth to a litter of kittens in April while *Titanic* was en route to Southampton. Jessop further added that Jenny and Jim were devoted to each other.

Jessop – who survived the sinking – was no stranger to seaborne disasters – she had previously survived the collision between *Titanic*'s sister ship, RMS *Olympic*, and HMS *Hawke* in 1911. As coincidence would have it, both Jessop and Jenny the cat were on board the *Olympic* at the time. Jessop also went on to survive the sinking of HMS *Britannic* in 1916. Due to this lucky streak she became known, perhaps rather macabrely, if not somewhat fittingly, as the Queen of Sinking Ships.

And so what then of Jim? Joseph Mulholland was indeed a crewmember on board *Titanic*, although he was a stoker rather than a kitchen hand, and he was the second person to corroborate the existence of Jenny and her disembarkation from *Titanic* before the ship sailed. Mulholland told his story several times over the years that followed the disaster, with considerable variation, but one of the most quoted of his remarks is preserved in a letter printed in the *Belfast News Letter*, 9 April 1964: 'I owe my life to a cat and an old superstition.'

Another potential reason for Mulholland deciding not to continue with *Titanic* was that of money: a better offer came along. In a later interview, Mulholland also alluded to the fact that it was actually a disagreement with a superior that led to him not remaining with *Titanic*.

According to Mulholland, however, it was ultimately Jenny leaving the ship that finally swung the decision for him. Junior boilermaker Hugh Fitzpatrick, a friend of Mulholland's who had been the one to suggest he stay with *Titanic*, was sadly not so fortunate, and died during the tragedy.

Despite the word of Jessop and Mulholland, there is debate regarding whether Jenny did in fact leave *Titanic* before she sailed, and if not, she sadly most likely went down with the ship, as there were no further sightings of her in the aftermath. In the wake of such a terrible tragedy, however, it is far preferable to imagine a happy ending for Jenny, and the legend of her life-saving premonition continues to this day.

TITANIC

Another feline said to have escaped a watery fate was Dowie, the ship's cat on the British ocean liner RMS *Lusitania.* According to legend, Dowie abandoned the liner on the night of 30 April 1915 – the night before she was due to leave New York for Liverpool on her 202nd voyage across the Atlantic.

On 7 May 1915, *Lusitania* was torpedoed and sunk by the German U-boat, *U-20*, resulting in the deaths of 1,198 people out of the 1,960 on board. Like Jenny before her, Dowie has been credited with saving lives – this time of several stokers – who thought the cat leaving was a bad omen and likewise abandoned the ship before she sailed.

The *Lusitania* herself had been instrumental in the rescue of the crew of the RMS *Mayflower* the previous year. With the ship drifting, rudderless and with a leaking hull, those on board were pulled by rope, one by one, from the *Mayflower* to the *Lusitania.* There were no human fatalities, but the ship's cat was sadly reported to have drowned, despite the best efforts of one of the crew to save it.

Emmy, the cat of the ocean liner RMS *Empress of Ireland*, is also famous for her survival instincts. On 28 May 1914, while the ship was in port in Quebec City, Canada, Emmy left the ship. Her departure was noticed by crew members who returned her to the boat, but Emmy refused to stay put; she absconded again – even leaving kittens behind on board – and the liner set sail without her.

In the early hours of 29 May, the Norwegian steam cargo ship, SS *Storstad*, hit the *Empress* in thick fog in the Gulf of St Lawrence, Canada. The *Empress of Ireland* sank, with 1,012 out of the 1,477 on board losing their lives. The sinking was the worst in Canadian history, and one of the greatest maritime disasters to take place during peacetime.

Cats generally haven't fared well when actually on board during a shipwreck, but one cat at least was well known for beating the odds: Unsinkable Sam. According to the lore that grew up around this remarkable feline, 'Sam' was actually a cat named Oscar. He was said to have escaped death not once, but an impressive three times during World War II, surviving the sinking of the German battleship *Bismarck*, British destroyer HMS *Cossack* and aircraft carrier HMS *Ark Royal*. 'Sam' rose to fame when on 14 November 1941, the *Ark Royal* was torpedoed a short distance from Gibraltar. She sank, but, according to an admiralty report two days later, there had only been one human fatality, and 'most of' the ship's cats had been rescued.

On 18 November, a Reuters story described how a black cat had been discovered in the water after the sinking, clinging to a plank from the wreckage. It was in this account that Oscar's incredible history was first related, and – although there is no hard evidence to link Oscar to the *Bismarck* or *Cossack* – he quickly captured the public imagination, becoming known by the moniker Unsinkable Sam.

After his *Ark Royal* adventure, however, 'Sam's' seafaring days were numbered: he was returned to the UK, where he sat out the rest of the war in a home for seamen in Belfast. He lived until 1955, making him at least an impressive 15 or 16 years old.

Cats and the Weather

The state of the weather has always been of utmost importance to humankind; our ability to adapt to and predict its sudden shifts and seemingly erratic impulses impacts our very survival. As a result, folklore and superstition are full of beliefs and ideas that reflect this necessary preoccupation.

Cats in particular, with their often seemingly preternatural abilities, have long been said to possess an ability to sense what the weather might hold, and even, in some cases, to be able to influence the weather itself.

Rain, Rain, Go Away

There exists a large body of folklore regarding animals and their ability to predict the weather: from cows lying down to croaking frogs, the creatures of the natural world can, according to popular belief, forecast everything from raging gales to brilliant sunshine. It is no surprise, therefore, to find that there is a wealth of such superstitions where the readily observable cat is concerned.

Many of these beliefs focus on how and when a cat washes itself, and the idea that a cat washing in a certain way can predict if the day will be foul or fair. One popular idea found in many places around the globe is that a cat washing itself means that bad weather will follow soon after. In areas of England in the 16th century, it was believed that if a cat was found sitting in the window enjoying the sunlight, licking itself with one of its feet behind an ear, it would be sure to rain that day. A cat licking its feet or putting its feet behind its head continued to be seen as a precursor to rain through the centuries that followed, and an 18th-century verse records this popular belief: 'Pussy a prophet too appears, against a rainy shower; She with her paws still cleans her ears, and then her face does scour.'

The idea that a cat washing behind its ear meant bad weather persisted into the 20th century. How hard the cat was washing was said to determine just how bad the weather would be: for example, if a cat washed behind its ears vigorously, then heavy rain could be expected. It was even said that the direction the wind would come from could be ascertained from the direction that the cat was facing.

Although they are keen self-cleaners, cats are generally less enthusiastic when it comes to being washed with water. In Indonesia there is a belief that you should think carefully before giving your feline friend a bath, as this will lead to great storms or even hurricanes. Leaving a cat to wash itself, however, can be fortuitous; it is said that a cat licking one foot means money coming your way.

A cat washing has also been said to predict things other than the weather; in England, an 18th-century superstition suggested that if a cat washed over its ear then a stranger would arrive. If it was the right ear, the visitor would be a man, while the left ear heralded the arrival of a woman – an idea that has continued into the 20th century and beyond. In Japan, likewise, if a cat washes its face with its paws, then visitors would soon be due.

Contrary to the general trend, a 19th-century belief from some areas of the USA stated that *good* weather could be expected when a cat washed itself. This only held true if it washed in a certain way, however, and it was important to pay attention to which direction the cat licked itself – if licking 'against the grain', washing its face over one ear or sitting with its back to the fire, then bad weather could be expected instead.

It wasn't just a cat's hygiene habits that were linked to bad weather; according to a 19th-century superstition, if a cat sat with its tail to the fire then a cold snap was coming and frost was on the way. A saying from England recorded in the mid-

20th century goes, 'Cat on its brain, it's going to rain', meaning that if a cat was resting with the flat part of its head pressed to the ground, then rain was sure to follow. Another belief suggests that when a cat's pupils widen then rain is imminent, and likewise if a cat sneezes it is going to rain. If the cat sneezes three times, however, then it is a sign that illness is coming to the house. In England, Holland, and elsewhere, if a cat was seen clawing at the curtains or carpet, then it was a sign that bad weather was on the way, while a belief from Ireland stated that if a cat was seen to be scraping at timber with its claws, then a storm should likewise be expected.

A traditional ritual found in north-east Thailand and some areas of Cambodia, *Hae Nang Maew* ('Procession of the Lady Cat') reflects the belief that cats cause droughts due to their dislike of water. It is performed during the drought season, between May and August, when rain is needed urgently for the crops. A cat – preferably cloud- or black-coloured – is placed in a lidded basket made from bamboo or rattan. This is then hung from a pole held between two people and the eldest person in attendance asks the cat to bring rain to ease the drought. The cat is processed about the area, accompanied by five pairs of candles, five pairs of flowers and a variety of instruments. As the parade passes, the people watching are asked to pour water on the cat, in the belief that it will end the drought as it does not like being wet. The ceremony is loud and boisterous, characterized by gongs, cymbals and singing, with the noise thought to encourage the cat to bring the rain. It is believed that rain will come within three to seven days of the ritual taking place.

Today, in Thailand, with an increased awareness of the well-being of the cat itself, in some areas significant changes have been made to the ceremony: the cat is replaced with a stuffed toy, or children and adults dress as cats themselves. Sometimes cats are made from bamboo frames and coconut husks as a replacement.

Is there any truth in this supposed connection between the behaviour of cats and the weather? It is said that cats – along with many other animals – are sensitive to fluctuations in atmospheric pressure, and other changes associated with an imminent shift in the weather, and that this might explain the link that has been made between the two.

It is thought that, due to their superior sense of smell, cats are able to scent incoming rain on the air long before our human senses have an inkling; likewise, with their sensitive hearing, they are able to pick up on sounds such as thunder or an increase in the wind before such changes are perceptible to their owners.

So, the next time you leave the house it may be wise to pay close attention to how your cat is behaving before you decide whether to take an umbrella with you or not!

Cats at Sea

One place in particular where keeping one step ahead of the weather has always been of utmost importance is at sea. Due to the widely perceived connection between cats and the weather, it is hardly surprising to discover that sailors and fishermen had strong beliefs where they were concerned, with firm taboos regarding cats both at sea and on land.

In general, cats were said to be bad luck on board a vessel and many sailors refused to take one out to sea. This extended in many cases to even saying the word 'cat' while at sea – or when travelling to it – for fear that doing so would place everyone in great danger.

There were exceptions, however, and a black cat on board was actually often considered to be *good* luck instead. Cats were even thought to provide protection at sea in some instances: in the Highlands of Scotland, for example, there was a belief that a cat on a boat would provide protection from witches. If a black cat was on board a ship and walked away from a sailor, then he would likely refuse to sail; this is linked to a more general belief that the front of a black cat brings good luck, while the back of the cat brings bad luck.

In Aberdeen, Scotland, people used the phrase 'We've met the cat' if a fishing trip had been unsuccessful and there had been a poor catch that day, or in general about any task that had not gone as well as expected.

In Somerset, in the south-west of England, sailors were generally wary of cats, and if they met a black cat on the way to their ship, they would turn around and go home, seeing it as a bad omen. In the Shetland Islands, off the north-east coast of Scotland, it was believed to be good luck if a cat ran before a fisherman when on his way to go fishing, although it was bad luck if the cat actually crossed his path.

In some areas such as Aberdeen, even saying the word 'cat' was believed to be unlucky; in the Shetland Islands during the 19th century, when fishermen were setting their lines, it was taboo to say the word 'cat' until they had finished. Cats were instead referred to as *kirser*, *fitting*, *vengler* or *foodin*.

Another long-held belief was that if a cat was observed running about being frisky, then storms and high winds could be expected. 'The cat has a gale of wind in her tail', was a popular saying, and an agitated cat on board ship was taken as a sign that bad weather was imminent. Of course, it made a difference if wind was needed or not, as to whether this was taken as bad luck or the opposite!

The belief that cats could predict the weather developed over time to include the idea that cats could actually influence the weather themselves. It was said that throwing a cat overboard or drowning it would bring on a storm, or even that the cat itself would summon bad weather in punishment for being cast into the water. In the 18th century it was said that drowning a cat would create a wind. It was therefore often held to be highly unlucky to cast a cat into the water while at sea. The cat's ability to influence the weather could also be a positive thing, however, as their wind-wielding powers could aid a ship or vessel that had been becalmed, and the throwing of a cat overboard or drowning one in order to summon a wind was sadly another common idea.

The storm-summoning properties of cats were said to be used by witches. Agnes Sampson, tried as a witch in 1591 in North Berwick, Scotland, confessed to several cat-related crimes with the intention of causing storms. According to sources, Agnes confessed to baptizing a cat before tying the bones of a human corpse to it. The cat was then cast into the sea by Agnes and her fellow witches, with the intention of raising a storm against King James VI as he travelled back from Denmark.

Shutting a cat up was also said to bring on storms: in the early 19th century, fishermen from Hauxley, Northumberland, in the north-east of England, would shut a cat inside a cupboard in the hope of summoning a wind. In 1831, naturalist Charles Darwin, writing in the diary of HMS *Beagle*, recorded how they were stuck in port, waiting for a favourable wind, and that the sailors were of the opinion that someone on shore was keeping a black cat under a tub, meaning they couldn't leave harbour. The belief that drowning or shutting up a cat could do this persisted well into the 20th century. In Castletown, County Limerick, Ireland, keeping a cat confined to cause storms was a common belief among sailors' wives. One was recorded jokingly remarking that she would put a cat under a pot in order to bring bad weather to keep her husband from being able to leave for sea again!

Lucky at Sea: Polydactyl Cats

Have you ever thought about the toes of a cat? In general they have 18 in total: five on each forepaw, four on each hindpaw. Sometimes however a cat is born with more than the expected number of digits, a condition known as polydactyly or polydactylism. The highest number of toes recorded on a single cat is 28 – two cats hold this record: Paws from America and Jake from Canada.

Polydactyl cats can be found in many areas of the world, but the greatest prevalence exists in the south-west of England and Wales and the east coast of North America – USA and Canada.

Polydactyl cats were, according to folklore, held in high esteem by sailors due to their reputed expertize in climbing and balancing. This led to them sometimes being referred to as 'ship's cats' and they were considered good luck which meant they were exempt from the often negative ideas regarding cats on board. This popularity at sea in turn contributed to the spread of polydactyl cats around the globe as they travelled from place to place.

Polydactyl cats are also sometimes referred to as 'Hemingway Cats' due to their association with the author Ernest Hemingway. Hemingway was gifted a six-toed cat by the captain of a ship, sparking a life-long love of the polydactyl. His former home in Key West, Florida, was turned into a museum upon his death in 1961 – and has remained a home for his cats and their descendants ever since. Today, approximately fifty cats live there, many of which are polydactyl.

Cats and Popular Sayings

Over the millennia, humankind has developed a wealth of idioms, proverbs and sayings in an attempt to explain and understand the world in which we live, with a phrase for almost every occasion and eventuality. As in so many other areas, cats feature prominently, highlighting yet again their unerring ability to infiltrate our lives. Such sayings also give an insight into how cats and their natures have been perceived across time and place, shedding further light on our beliefs and ideas regarding these most favoured of companions.

Curiosity Killed the Cat and Other Idioms

One highly popular cat-related saying is the proverbial 'Curiosity killed the cat'. Cats have a reputation for getting into mischief and sticking their noses and paws into things they should leave well alone, and this familiar proverb warns against following their example.

The oldest variation of the saying is actually 'Care killed the cat' – with 'care' meaning 'sorrow for others' or 'worry'. This version was known as early as the late 16th century, and is referenced in Ben Jonson's play *Every Man in His Humour*, dating to 1598: 'Helter skelter, hang sorrow, care'll kill a cat.' The 1898 edition of *Brewer's Dictionary of Phrase and Fable* includes an entry saying that, 'It is said that a cat has nine lives, but care would wear them all out', which is also possibly linked to this.

A Handbook of Proverbs (1873) by James Allan Mair attributes 'Curiosity killed the cat' as an Irish proverb. Variants in the 20th century include, 'Curiosity killed a cat, but it came back', as recorded in Texas, USA, in 1905, and 'Curiosity killed the cat; but satisfaction brought it back'.

'While the cat's away, the mice will play' is another saying with an old provenance, dating back to the mid-1400s, meaning that when those in charge or authority are absent, their subordinates will misbehave or not do as they are supposed to. It comes from the Latin *Dum felis dormit, mus gaudet et exsi litantro*, which translates literally as, 'When the cat sleeps, the mouse leaves its hole, rejoicing'. A widespread concept, there are variants of this saying in several languages, including Russian, French, German and Spanish.

Another popular phrase is the question, 'Cat got your tongue?' often used when a person isn't speaking especially when it comes to children. There are several weird and wonderful theories regarding the origins of this saying, including the idea that ancient kings would cut out the tongues of dissenters and feed them to their cats, or that sailors would be struck silent by the threat of being whipped by the highly feared cat o'nine tails. There is no evidence to support such claims, however, and the phrase is thought to actually be of relatively recent origin, perhaps as late as the late 19th century.

The word 'cat' itself has, over time, had several meanings and connotations. In England, 'cat' was a slang term for a prostitute from at least 1400, and even before that was used as a general term of contempt for a woman. It was also used to refer to a 'cross old woman' by at least the 18th century, and the term 'cat-witted' dates back to the 17th century, meaning obstinate, spiteful and small-minded.

To turn 'cat in pan' refers to changing sides or parties in an argument or a political setting, while to live under the 'cat's foot' was used to describe a man who was said to be living under the control of his wife, akin to being 'hen-pecked'. Due to the naturally tempestuous relationship between the two animals, 'To live like dog and cat' referred to married couples who lived unhappily together.

The cunning nature of the cat is noted in the term 'cat's sleep', alluding to the fact that cats often feign sleep in order to lure their prey closer before pouncing on them. 'Cat burglar', also pays homage to the cat's wily ways, referring to their stealth and ability to move about undetected, and has been in use from the early 20th century. To 'cat' or 'shoot the cat', meant to vomit from drunkenness or an excess of liquor.

The saying 'Belling the cat' or 'Bell the cat' references the fact that it is easy to propose a solution to a problem, but not so easy to actually carry it out in practice. It is said to originate from a tale attributed to Aesop of the same name, where a council of mice gather to discuss how they are going to deal with the cat, the enemy of all mice. The mice make many suggestions, none of which are accepted, until finally a young mouse suggests that the best idea would be to attach a bell to a ribbon and place this around the neck of the cat, so that they would always be able to hear it coming.

All of the mice agree that it is an ingenious plan. The celebration is short-lived, however, as an older, wiser mouse raises an important point: who among them will actually carry out the plan and put the bell on the cat?

The mice look from one to another, and it quickly becomes clear that none of them are willing or able to actually do it, having all assumed that some other mouse would volunteer, highlighting the crucial importance of considering how a plan will be carried out in practice, not just in theory.

Although the story is attributed to Aesop, from the tales known as *Aesop's Fables*, dating from the 6th century BCE, there is actually no record of this particular story before medieval times, with one of the earliest attested versions dating to 1200 CE. The tale was popular, however, and was translated into various languages including Welsh, French and Spanish, and was also used as a handy metaphor in various political situations.

In Japan, *Neko o kaburu* ('To put a cat on') means to pretend to be quiet and nice, putting on a mask around those you are wary of or trying to fool. *Neko no te mo karitai* ('Even wants to borrow a cat's paws') is a term used to express that someone is so busy they would take any help available, regardless of how little use it might actually be.

The Dutch *As ons ka teen koei was, honnen we ze melken veu de stoof* ('If your cat was a cow, we could milk it in front of the hearth') is a wonderfully evocative response to someone who starts a sentence with a hypothetical 'if', highlighting the futility of pointless speculation when trying to decide what to do in a given situation. *Okači mačku o rep* ('Hang it on a cat's tail') is a saying used in Serbia, Bosnia and Montenegro, to refer to an action by someone that you consider to be useless.

Il n'y a pas un chat ('There isn't a cat') is a French term used to describe a place that is entirely empty; so empty, in fact that there isn't even a cat there. *Avoir d'autres chats à fouetter* ('Having other cats to whip') is another French phrase, meaning having better things to do, and is said to date from the 17th century.

Letting the Cat Out of the Bag

Meaning to accidentally reveal a big secret that has thus far been kept hidden, this saying has often been attributed to nautical origins. The prevailing theory suggests that the 'cat' involved refers to the cat o'nine tails, the nine-'tailed' whip used to enforce discipline on board ship. This 'cat' was stored in a bag, and so it would be 'let out' when it was removed for use. Unfortunately for this highly popular theory, however, there is no evidence that the cat o'nine tails was regularly stored in this fashion.

This saying has also been linked to the phrase 'To buy a pig [or, in this case, a cat] in a poke [bag]'. This older saying, said to date from the 16th century, meant 'To buy a thing without looking at it or enquiring into its value', only to reach home to discover that it was a cat instead.

Another phrase connected to the nautical 'cat' is 'Not enough room to swing a cat'. Once again, this is said to relate to the cat o'nine tails, which would need a significant amount of space to be wielded properly – space that was decidedly lacking below decks on a ship. However, it is likely that this seafaring connection came later, as the saying is attested to as early as 1665, with no known nautical connection.

Raining Cats and Dogs

Heavy rain – sometimes dreaded, sometimes longed for – occurs to a greater or lesser extent across most areas of the world. As a result, many phrases have developed to describe this phenomenon, often involving animals. According to an Afrikaans expression it is raining frogs and toads, while in Germany young dogs fall from the sky, with a Portugese saying from Brazil warning of snakes and lizards.

The most common phrase to describe a sudden downpour in England and the United States is 'raining cats and dogs'.

The earliest recorded instance of the concept comes from 1651 in Welsh poet and author Henry Vaughan's collection of poems, *Olor Iscanus*: 'dogs and cats rained in shower'. The following year, the line 'it shall rain dogs and polecats' appeared in Richard Brome's 1652 play *The City Witt* – although a polecat is in fact a member of the weasel family and not a feline.

There are various theories for where this phrase originated; as always with such things, some hold more weight than others. One rather unsanitary idea is that it reflects the poor state of drainage in 17th-century Europe, and is referenced in Jonathan Swift's 1710 poem, 'Description of a City Shower'. According to this theory, when there was a sudden downpour dead animals – largely cats and dogs – would be swept along and float down the street:

Drowned puppies, stinking sprats, all drenched in mud,
Dead cats, and turnip tops, come tumbling down the flood.

Another idea is that the idiom stems from the Greek phrase *kata doksa*, which roughly translates as something that is 'contrary to expectations'. It has also been suggested that it is a corruption of the Greek word *Katadoupoi* or *Κατάδουποι* which refers to the waterfalls on the River Nile. Consequently, Old French and Old English for waterfall is *catadupe*.

Cats feature in similar phrases in other countries: the Flemmish saying *het regent kattenjongen* means 'it's raining kittens', whereas in Norway it is said to be snowing kittens.

Witches and Cats

For centuries, cats have been linked with magic and witchcraft in the popular imagination. This has, for the most part, been a decidedly negative connection, leading to cats being greatly maligned through the ages and often treated with suspicion and distrust.

Whether directly assisting a witch in their destructive behaviour or unwittingly aiding such maleficium by being used in spells, cat and witch became inextricably linked, a bond that, once forged, proved much harder to break.

The Witch's Cat

It is often said that hatred for the humble cat was largely due to the passing in 1233 of the papal bull *Vox in Rama*, by Pope Gregory IX. According to popularly held belief, this document named cats as vile and demonic relics of paganism, and resulted in the mass persecution of cats throughout Christendom. But the truth, as is often the case, isn't quite so clear cut. The bull was in fact dealing with a specific sect in Germany that was said to, among other things, kiss the buttocks of a statue of a black cat that represented their master, as part of their worship. Although not primarily aimed at demonizing cats, the bull had the knock-on effect of doing just that – though there is no evidence for the mass cat-culling that is often said to have resulted.

Although there were earlier such connections, cats became irrevocably linked with witches and witchcraft from the 16th century onwards, and the advent of the witch trials that swept across Europe and parts of colonial America. During this time – and beyond – witches were believed to have familiar spirits that did their bidding; in England, these were often said to take the form of animals, and the cat was the most popular of these demonic helpers.

The first trial in England to result in the execution of an individual for witchcraft included one such animal. In 1566, Agnes Waterhouse of Hatfield Peverel, Essex, confessed to causing death and harm to several people and animals through acts of witchcraft, which were aided by her familiar, the aptly named Satan or Satan the cat.

According to Agnes's confession, Satan was a white cat that had been gifted to her by Elizabeth Francis, another woman accused of witchcraft, who had, in turn, received the animal from her grandmother. Elizabeth herself had used the cat to free herself from an abusive husband and to get revenge on those who had argued with her in the village, and now Agnes could do the same. All Agnes had to do was give the cat some milk to drink and the occasional drop of blood, and then the cat would do her bidding.

According to her confession, Agnes used the cat to kill one of her own hogs as a test; when this was successful, she went on to order the death of three hogs belonging to a Father Kersey. When they died, she rewarded Satan with a chicken and a drop of her own blood. Emboldened by this success, Agnes then used the cat to drown the cow of a woman she had an argument with, and three geese of another, and also confessed to destroying the brewing and butter of other locals, among a variety of other malefic acts. Agnes was found guilty of using witchcraft to kill a man, and was convicted and hanged on 29 July 1566.

From this time onwards, cats increasingly appeared in various forms throughout records of the witch trials in England, carrying out a variety of acts from causing illness to outright murder. In the case of the Belvoir Witches from Leicestershire, England, Joan Flower and her daughters Philippa and Margaret were accused of bewitching to death the sons of the Earl of Rutland and his wife. Among other methods, they confessed to taking a glove that belonged to one of the children, dipping it in boiling water, rubbing it along the back of their cat, Rutterkin, and then pricking it. Although this was seen as successful against the boys, it transpired that the familiar didn't have the power to harm the couple's daughter, Katherine.

Witches were also said to be able to transform their shape, and often this was into that of a cat. Isobel Gowdie, convicted of witchcraft in Auldearn, Scotland in 1662, confessed that she and her fellow witches recited the following words three times in order to do so:

I shall go into a cat,
With sorrow and such and a little black shot.
And I shall go in the Devil's name,
Ay while I come home again.

Having cats around, or them being seen outside a house, therefore was also said to be a sign of witchcraft. Sometimes cats were even said to talk; Jane Wenham, the last woman to be convicted of witchcraft in England in 1712, said that cats had talked to her, and in 1718, William Montgomerie from Scotland declared that his house was filled with cats that talked to each other and that he couldn't stay there any longer. When it came to magic itself, cats were said to be used in a variety of cures and spells.

Today, the historical link between witches and cats remains deeply ingrained in our collective consciousness. In children's books and art work, television and Halloween decorations, the witch and the cat are, forever, inextricably linked.

Cat Saints and Feline Deities

Cats have been both revered and reviled across many belief systems throughout history, seen as both deity and demon and everything in between. From feline gods and goddesses to cat saints and their legends, from ancient Egypt to 20th century Spain, cats have held a prominent and complex position in our beliefs down through the millennia.

Bastet and the Sun God: Cats in Ancient Egypt

In ancient Egyptian society, certain animals were seen to be a representation of a particular god or goddess. Cats, due to their general popularity, which peaked during the Ptolemaic period (332–330 BCE), were prominent in various Egyptian myths and art, and were associated with several feline deities.

Perhaps the best known of these was the goddess Bastet. The primary deity of the city of Bubastis, located in the eastern Nile delta, her name means literally, 'She of the city of Bast'. According to some sources, the goddess was also referred to as Bubastis, further confirming her connection to the city.

The earliest extant representations of Bastet show a woman with a lioness's head: with a *uraeus* or serpent on her forehead, she holds a long sceptre in one hand and an *ankh* – a sign meaning life – in the other. Over time, domestic cats started to be seen as a manifestation of Bastet, and the goddess eventually began to be shown as a cat, or a woman with a cat's head, a transition that took place during the first millennium BCE.

Said to be one of the daughters of Ra, the sun god, over time Bastet became closely linked with several other Egyptian goddesses, including Mut (who was sometimes also shown as a lion-headed figure), Hathor and Isis.

Although the best known today, Bastet wasn't the first feline-headed goddess in ancient Egypt: the earliest was probably the goddess known as Mafdet. Mafdet is mentioned in the *Pyramid Texts*, the oldest extant body of ancient Egyptian religious texts inscribed upon the walls and sarcophagi of pyramids at Saqqara, dating to c. 2400–2300 BCE. Here, Mafdet is represented as a panther, and is shown killing venomous snakes and other enemies of the sun god. In a vignette from the *Book of the Dead*, dating from around 1650 BCE, a goddess is depicted in scenes of judgement upon a deceased individual: generally nameless, it is thought that this may in fact also be Mafdet in panther form, and it has been suggested that the earlier representations of Mafdet were forerunners of the goddess Bastet.

The lion-headed goddess Sekhmet likewise had close links to Bastet. Although Sekhmet and Bastet were originally both depicted in this way, they developed their own distinct aspects: in keeping with the Egyptian characteristic of understanding a concept as two opposite extremes, Sekhmet represented the lion-like aspect of the feline personality and Bastet the domestic cat. This fact is demonstrated clearly in the description of Hathor-Tefnut in *The Myth of the Eye of the Sun*, which says: 'She rages like Sekhmet and she is friendly like Bastet,' highlighting the perceived characteristics of both the war-like lion and the domestic feline that were associated with each deity.

Another lioness goddess was the evocatively named Pakhet. Her name, from *pakh* ('to scratch'), means 'She who scratches', and evidence for belief in the goddess is present from the Middle Kingdom period (c. 2040–1782 BCE) onwards. Pakhet is mentioned in spell 470 of the *Coffin Texts*:

I have appeared as Pakhet the Great,
whose eyes are keen and whose claws are sharp,
the lioness who sees and catches by night.

Bastet was closely associated with nurturing instincts and childbearing, a feature she shared with several other goddesses that manifested as lionesses or cats. The two sides to Bastet – and indeed the cat she is represented by – are clearly reflected in some statuettes of the goddess: the ferocious hunter suggested by her lion's head, while the softer, nurturing characteristics are implied by the small domestic cat at her side.

Like some of his daughters, the sun god Ra himself had strong links with the cat, and it is clear that he could and did at times appear in cat form. In spell 335 of the *Coffin Texts*, dating from c. 2100 BCE, it says of Ra: 'I am the Great Tom Cat/Miuoa' and then, even more explicitly, 'this Great Tom cat was the god Ra himself'. Ra also appears in cat form twice in the *Litany of the Sun*, where 75 names of the sun god are given: two such names are Miuty and the Great Tom Cat.

There is also archaeological evidence that Ra took a cat's form or was represented by a cat, including the second gold shrine of Tutankhamun (1336–1327 BCE), where Ra is shown with a cat's head; the Tomb of Nakhtamun, where a cat is described as 'great cat, a form of the god Ra'; and also on some *stelae* – stone slabs erected as a monument of commemoration – from the Ramesside period (c. 1295–1070 BCE) in connection with the sun god.

In the *Book of the Dead*, a vignette accompanying spell 17 that is closely related to spell 335 from the *Coffin Texts* mentioned above, also features a cat-headed Ra. It was believed that at night the sun god had to travel through the underworld, going through a series of challenges there before emerging into the world again to bring the sun of the new day.

There, in cat form, Ra is shown fighting and killing his enemy Apep, a serpent that is the representation of darkness and chaos. Ra is ultimately triumphant, and the sun reappears in the skies the following morning with life continuing afresh.

The important position the cat held within Egyptian society is also reflected in the choice of names used across the period, and there are many cat-related examples. Children, for example, were often named after animals, and 'Miut' or 'Miit', along with the later 'Ta-Muit', meaning female cat, are noted among recognized names of the period. A servant woman named Miut is recorded on a gravestone of an individual from Giza (c. 2311–2140 BCE) with the name containing a hieroglyph of a cat either crouching or lying. Another example is the grave of a five-year-old girl named Miit or Myt from the household of King Mentuhotep II (c. 2050–1994 BCE), which depicts a cat seated with its tail curling up across its back. Cats even influenced royalty: a king from the twenty-second Dynasty (c. 945–715 BCE) was called Pamiu – the Tom Cat.

Cat Gods and Goddesses

Ancient Egypt was far from the only culture to have feline-related gods and goddesses, and a variety of feline deities can be found throughout history.

TEZCATLIPOCA

The Aztec god Tezcatlipoca was closely associated with the night sky, magic, war and death. Said to manifest in a variety of forms, including that of a large black jaguar in which he was known as Tepeyollotl or Mountain Heart, Tezcatlipoca is sometimes listed as one of the four sons of the primordial dual deity, Ometecuhtli and Omecihuatl. Tezcatlipoca is also closely associated with obsidian mirrors; his name is often translated as a 'smoking mirror', an allusion to this connection.

It is believed that Tezcatlipoca may have had origins in earlier Mesoamerican deities from the Olmec or Maya cultures, both of which also had a jaguar deity among their pantheons. Tezcatlipoca may therefore have been a continuation of these gods, or was built on their foundations.

In appearance, in his non-jaguar form, Tezcatlipoca is largely identified by his prominent face paint of horizontal stripes in black and yellow. Tezcatlipoca is also depicted with a headdress of feathers and flowers, flint knives, heron feathers and balls of eagle down. Clearly identified as a warrior god, he is depicted with both shield and breastplate, with an arrow for a nose ring and spears and arrows about his person. Some texts present the god as being close to invisible, due to his links with darkness and his omnipresent nature.

In one of the Aztec creation stories, before the world was created, there existed only the sea, and, dwelling within it, the primordial monster of the earth, Cipactli. In order to create the world, gods Quetzalcoatl and Tezcatlipoca used Tezcatlipoca's foot as bait to lure Cipactli from the depths: the ruse worked, and the gods captured her, twisting and pulling her body in order to create the land. When people were created, they were instructed to make regular sacrifices to Cipactli, in order to comfort her and to recognize her great sacrifice. In reference to this story, Tezcatlipoca is often depicted with one foot missing, the appendage variously replaced with a bone, serpent or mirror.

How did Tezcatlipoca come to be a jaguar? According to the Aztec sacred story 'The Five Suns', the god turned himself into the sun. Greatly angered, Quetzalcoatl used a stone club to hit Tezcatlipoca from the sky. Furious at this treatment, Tezcatlipoca transformed into a jaguar, and in turn destroyed the world.

Tezcatlipoca's main feast was Toxcatl, which took place during the fifth month of the Aztec calendar.

NARASIMHA

The Hindu deity Narasimha, literally translated from the Sanskrit as 'man-lion', is the fourth *avatara* or incarnation of the Hindu god Vishnu, one of the principal deities in the Hindu pantheon. In appearance, the god has a curly mane, lion-like features and sharp, curved teeth. With a human body, he has a thick neck, large shoulders and a broad abdomen, tapering off to a slender waist. Narasimha also goes by several other names, including Kala, Parakala or Mahakala, 'the one who has a wide mouth and projecting teeth', 'the one who killed Hiranyakashipu', 'the one who has a lion face', 'the one who is a lion', and 'the one for whom nails are his weapons'. He is also known as the god of destruction and the Great Protector. Within Vaishnavism – one of the four main forms of Hinduism – Vishnu is the most important of the Hindu deities and the ultimate manifestation of the divine.

Narasimha is mentioned in the Hindu sacred book the Rig Veda, including hymn 1.154 dating to 1700–1200 BCE. Vishnu, in the form of Narashima, is described as 'wild lion, powerful, prowling, mountain-roaming'. Representations of Narashima exist from at least the 4th century CE.

One of the most popular stories involving Narasimha is that of his defeat of the demon king Hiranyakashipu. Hiranyakashipu wanted revenge against Vishnu for killing his brother Hiranyaksha while the god was in the third of his ten incarnations, and it is through this story that Narasimha is credited with ending religious persecution and restoring dharma – calmness – to the world.

Hiranyakashipu performed penance for several years, and in return, was granted a boon – that is a favour or blessing granted by a deity, usually in exchange for devotion or penance by an individual – by the god Brahma. In this way, Hiranyakashipu gained the powers he needed to carry out his plan of revenge.

He asked of Brahma that he would not be able to die either inside or outside of a residence, during the daytime or night time, or on the ground or in the sky. Furthermore, that his death would not be caused by either weapons or hands, or by a human being or an animal, or, even, by any being or thing, living or non-living, that had been created by the god. To further cement his safety, he also added that he couldn't even be killed by any organism or divinity.

Brahma granted this wish, and, satisfied that he had ensured his own survival, Hiranyakashipu was free to act as he pleased. His next step was to target those who worshipped and followed Vishnu, safe in the knowledge he could do so with impunity due to his own invincibility.

Emboldened, Hiranyakashipu didn't even hold back where his own son, Prahlada, was concerned: Prahlada had rebelled against his father, and had in turn become a devotee of his enemy Vishnu, and Hiranyakashipu wanted to punish him for this betrayal. Prahlada declared that Vishnu was omnipresent and lord of all, rather than his father, and this angered Hiranyakashipu so much that he was determined to kill him, and the boy was saved only by the intervention of Vishnu himself.

Still trying to sway his son, Hiranyakashipu pointed to a pillar. 'Was Vishnu even within that?', he demanded mockingly. For although Prahlada spoke so freely of a god who was above everything and was everywhere, where was he then at that moment?

The faithful Prahlada, unswayable as ever, simply told his father, 'He was. He is. He will be.'

Enraged, Hiranyakashipu smashed the pillar with a hard blow of his mace. Suddenly there came a loud sound and Vishnu – as Narasimha – appeared to defend Prahlada. Narasimha desired greatly to kill Hiranyakashipu, but needed to do so in such a way as to not violate the boon granted by Brahma.

But Vishnu was clever and cunning. He had chosen the form of Narasimha for this exact reason: in this form, he was neither a human, nor a deity or an animal, being part human and part animal, so therefore not fully either. Furthermore, it was twilight when he attacked – neither night nor day. The location was also carefully chosen, the perfect spot, the threshold of a courtyard, neither inside nor outside. There,

Narasimha placed the demon across his lap – in a place neither on earth nor space. For the killing blow, Narasimha likewise didn't break the boon granted by Brahma – with his blade-sharp fingernails – not animate or inanimate – he disembowelled Hiranyakashipu, killing the demon.

Narasimha, however, was so enraged that, even with the death of Hiranyakashipu, his ire was still not quenched, and the god continued on, untamed, putting the entire world in great danger. To combat this new threat, the other gods and goddesses intervened, sending Prahlada to sooth and calm Narasimha. Prahlada prayed to Narasimha, and the man-lion was pacified and once again became calm and in control of himself.

The god's victory is celebrated in the festival of Narasimha Jayanti, taking place during the month of Vaisakha (April and May). In the temple towns of Andhra Pradesh, Orissa and Tami Nadu, there are theatre performances that celebrate Narasimha.

A CHARIOT PULLED BY CATS: THE GODDESS FREYA

Goddess of fertility, love, beauty, war, the domestic sphere and female sexuality, the goddess Freya was one of the primary deities in the Norse pantheon. Daughter of the sea god Njord and Mother Earth goddess Nerthus or Herta, and twin sister to Freyr, god of fertility, peace and good weather, Freya is commonly depicted travelling in a chariot drawn by two large feline creatures: but where does this enduring and popular image originate?

The only mention of Freya's oversized felines in the original Norse sources is from the 13th-century *Prose Edda*: 'When she goes abroad, she drives in a car drawn by two cats.' This evocative description – however brief – nonetheless inspired countless depictions throughout the centuries that followed, and has become central to the imagery associated with the goddess today. There are various later interpretations and ideas regarding Freya and her faithful felines that have been embraced as canon where the goddess is concerned.

One popular tale, said to be of Russian origin, states that Thor, Norse god of thunder, gave the cats to the goddess. In this story, Thor was fishing one day, when a magical and beautiful singing sent him into a deep slumber. Suddenly a terrible noise woke him, and upon investigating, Thor discovered Cat Bayun – the popular trickster figure from Slavic folklore – singing to two sleeping blue-grey kittens. Cat Bayun revealed that the mother of the kittens had left him, and asked Thor for help. Thor agreed, and solved the issue by taking the kittens as a gift for Freya. Happy with this arrangement, Bayun transformed into a bird and flew off.

Freya's cats have often been given the names Tregul (meaning 'tree-gold' or 'amber') and Bygul (meaning 'bee-gold' or 'honey'). These names, however, come from the popular 1984 novel *Brisingamen* by Diana L Paxson: in the original sources, the cats are unnamed.

There has been some debate whether the creatures pulling Freya's chariot were originally cats at all. A 19th-century theory suggested that, originally, Freya's vehicle was actually drawn by two bears, and that confusion had arisen over the word *fres* or *fressum* being used to describe the creatures that pulled the goddess. According to this idea, the term meant both 'bear' and 'Tom cat' in Old Norse, and the use of *köttum* – 'cat' – might have been a later change introduced by Icelandic translators due to the fact that bears were not common to Iceland. Although taken up by Jacob Grimm, the idea gained little traction and today it is generally accepted that Freya's chariot was originally pulled by large cat or leonine creatures, perhaps lynx, tigers or even the non-feline marten.

Freya wasn't the only goddess to be depicted with a carriage drawn by felines of some sort. Cybele, a Roman fertility goddess known as Lady of the Animals, also rode in a carriage pulled by a pair of lions.

Ceridwen and Other Goddesses

Several goddesses, although not originally linked with cats in any way, have, over time, come to have strong feline connections.

The Welsh goddess Ceridwen, associated today with rebirth, inspiration and transformation, is frequently said to have had white cats attending her, carrying out her bidding. However, the earliest sources for the goddess make no mention of these feline companions, suggesting that they are a later invention.

The Greek goddess Artemis was sometimes equated with the Egyptian Bastet, and has become associated with cats due to this. Artemis, in turn, has been likewise linked with her Roman counterpart, Diana - both were known as the Lady of Animals. Ovid's *Metamorphoses* includes a story where the gods flee to Egypt, taking on animal form: Diana transforms into a cat.

The Greek Hekate, although today closely tied to witchcraft and magic, is also said to have had an association with cats; this has been a relatively modern development, influenced perhaps in part by her later association with Artemis.

The Cat on the Ark and Other Legends

Although there is some mention of larger felines such as lions and leopards, domestic cats are conspicuously absent from the Bible. However, in *The Gospel of Twelve*, part of the Christian Apocrypha, a collection of texts not included in the canonical New Testament, Jesus displays kindness towards cats on two occasions. He is shown driving off youths who were cruelly tormenting a cat, and on another occasion he is said to have picked up a cat that was lost and alone, sheltering it within his clothing to keep it warm and giving it food and drink.

Diverging from the biblical account of the birth of Jesus, in this gospel, a cat also makes an appearance together with the more commonly cited animals around the manger: 'And there were in the same cave an ox and a horse and an ass and a sheep, and beneath the manger was a cat with her little ones.'

The cat fares better within Islam and is mentioned in a positive light in various sources. According to Islamic legend, before the great flood the cat didn't exist at all and was in fact created on the Ark itself, in response to a very particular problem experienced by those on board. The vessel was overrun with a plague of rats: eating and spoiling food, chewing through clothes and fabric, they left destruction – and their waste – everywhere in their wake.

In response to the growing complaints, Noah approached the lion, running his hand down the majestic animal's back. The lion sneezed, and from his nose popped the cat; the newly created creature wasted no time dealing with the rats and the problem was solved.

In the Quran itself, lions and other larger animals stopped the Ark from being swamped by the 'ungodly', rushing to take cover when the flood became obvious.

Also within Islam, there are several stories relating to the prophet Muhammad and cats. One popular tale refers to a pet said to be much treasured by Muhammad, a cat named Muezza. One day Muezza was asleep on the prophet's sleeve, leaving him in a dilemma to which most cat owners can relate: not wanting to disturb a cat in order to go about his day. The solution, however, was close at hand: instead of waking his sleeping pet, the prophet carefully cut off his sleeve to leave it with the slumbering animal.

There is no evidence for this story in the original sources or known events of the prophet's life. This heart-warming tale appears to be a later attribution, but it is a reflection of the fact that cats were, and remain, highly regarded within Islam.

How the Tabby Got its Markings

The term 'tabby' refers not to a specific breed of cat, but to a particular coat pattern that can be found across many breeds of domestic feline. A tabby pattern is characterized by markings in the form of stripes, dashes or even spots, along with a distinctive 'M' on the cat's forehead. There are many stories and ideas to explain how this marking came about.

One idea is that the 'M' dates back to the birth of Jesus. There are variations on this tale, but the general theme is that a tender-hearted mother cat climbed into the manger to warm the chilly infant. When Mary saw this kindness, she reached down to stroke the cat's forehead, and the 'M' there is in memory of Mary touching it in thanks.

Another story traces the marking to a courageous act by Muezza, said to be the favoured pet of the prophet Muhammed. It is said that Muezza saved the prophet from a snake, and that because of this and her general faithfulness, Muhammed marked her with an 'M' that tabby cats have worn ever since.

There are other varied and imaginative theories regarding the origin of this distinctive feature, ranging from 'M' denoting 'moon' due to cats having a connection to this celestial body, to the idea that it in fact stands for 'mau', the Egyptian word for cat. One thing is for certain: however it came to be, the tabby 'M' is one of the most familiar cat markings of all.

Patrons of Cats: St Jerome and Other Cat Saints

St Jerome in his study kept a great big cat,
It's always in his pictures, with its feet upon the mat.
Did he give it milk to drink, in a little dish?
When it came to Fridays, did he give it fish?
If I lost my little cat, I'd be sad without it;
I should ask St Jerome what to do about it.
I should ask St Jerome, just because of that,
for he's the only saint I know who kept a kitty cat.
POPULAR RHYME, DATE AND AUTHOR UNKNOWN

When it comes to saints, it is widely known that St Christopher is the patron saint of travellers, and St Patrick offers protection against snakes. But is there a saint specifically associated with our faithful feline friends?

The patron saint of archaeologists, biblical scholars, librarians, students and translators, St Jerome is often linked with cats. This connection appears to have come about largely due to the fact that the saint was often depicted with a lion, an allusion to the popular legend regarding the saint removing a thorn from a lion's paw. It is said that the lion was so grateful for his aid that it stayed with Jerome from then on, becoming his faithful companion.

The lion features in several works of art, including the 15th-century painting *St Jerome in his Study* by Antonello da Messina, where the lion can be seen to one side of the saint, while a smaller domestic cat sits to the other side. A copper engraving of the same name by Albrecht Dürer (1514) again depicts the lion, this time at the saint's feet. It might be that the lion was misinterpreted as a typical house cat, and that, over time, the two became conflated.

Although there is no official patron saint of cats, St Gertrude of Nivelles – often cited as being their official protector – comes closest to fulfilling this role. This accolade, however, is a modern one; the first recorded mention explicitly linking Gertrude with cats dates back only to the 1980s.

How then did this transformation come about? Although her designation as the cat saint is a modern one, it seems that Gertrude was known for her power over rats and mice from at least the early 15th century, when she was held to be a protector against such vermin in the Netherlands, Catalonia, Spain, and south-west Germany. Over time, this connection extended to being associated with cats – those habitual enemies of rats and mice – and thus the patron saint of cats was born.

Another possible explanation for Gertrude's link to cats involves her connection with souls in purgatory. In medieval art, such souls were depicted as mice, and Gertrude, said to aid them, was often shown with mice around her feet. It has been suggested that this led to the connection between the saint and mice and, over time, her link with cats for which she is known today. There are reports that figures of gold mice were left at her shrine in Cologne, Germany, until the first quarter of the 19th century.

Today, Gertrude is remembered on 17 March, the date of her death, sharing her saint's day with the iconic St Patrick. She is also known as patron saint of travellers due to one of the miracles associated with her – she is said to have saved a group of sailors from a vicious sea monster.

Another saint with feline connections is St Agatha of Sicily. Martyred in the 3rd century CE, Agatha has come to be known as the patron saint of breast cancer patients, rape victims, bakers and nurses, natural disasters, earthquakes and fire. Her connection with cats is actually accidental, and comes from a misunderstanding of the pronunciation of Agatha's name. In the *Langue d'Oc*, a dialect of Occitan, the medieval language of the Languedoc region of France, the pronunciation of 'Agatha' is the same as *gato*, the Spanish and Italian for 'cat'. This has led to stories, particularly in the south of France, where the saint is portrayed with connections to cats, or even turning into a cat herself.

On St Agatha's Day – 5 February – work was prohibited, and no washing or spinning were to take place. According to traditional belief, it was said in some areas of the lower Pyrenees that if this taboo was broken, then offenders would be harshly punished by the saint. Among the various stories, some involve Agatha's connection with cats, and go something like this:

On St Agatha's Day, a woman from the village declared that she was going to go and start her washing. Her neighbour, rightly horrified, reminded her that this was a bad idea, for it was St Agatha's Day, and washing was forbidden.

The woman was unimpressed, crying out:

'Santo Gato gatara e la ruscado se fara,' or 'Saint Cat shall kitten and I shall have my wash.'

These were rash words indeed, for as the woman started to wash her clothes, a cat-like creature suddenly appeared at the chimney corner.

'Empty it, empty it!' cried the creature, when the cauldron needed to be emptied.

The woman was terrified, and ran to the neighbour who had warned her against washing. How she should have listened! Her friend gave her further good advice, and counselled her to go to the window when it was time to empty the final cauldron of water, and as she did so to shout out:

'The cemetery is on fire!'

The woman followed these instructions and the cat howled loudly, 'To my little home!' and dashed from the house.

The woman was much relieved, but a while later, however, the cat returned. The woman had, according to the cat, had a very lucky escape indeed. The cat, it was said, was none other than the saint herself, come from the grave to dole out punishment for not observing her day properly.

In another version, recorded from the Basque country between France and Spain, the offending woman is making bread. When a cat enters the house and steals a piece of the dough, the woman shouts at it to get out. The woman lives to regret this, however, as the cat speaks, announcing that she is not a cat but is, in fact, St Agatha herself. Looking up, as instructed by the cat, the woman discovers that her house is on fire in punishment for working on Agatha's day.

In some areas, it was still believed that there would be punishment for spinning on the saint's day until at least the mid-20th century.

The Cat and the Mouse: Lomasa and Palita

Cats find their way everywhere. This story is taken from the *Mahabharata*, one of the two main Sanskrit epics from ancient India. Belived to be the longest epic poem ever written, at approximately 1.8 million words, it covers both devotional and philosophical themes and is revered as a Smṛti text in Hinduism.

Once, a large banyan tree grew in the middle of a huge forest. As is their wont, the tree had a large trunk, with many, many branches reaching in each and every direction, with creepers and leaves aplenty to house all manner of wildlife, with both birds and animals making their homes there.

Beneath the banyan it was shady and cool, and it was here that a little mouse named Palita – much wiser than you might expect a mouse to be – made his home at the foot of the great old tree.

Higher up the tree, among the wide, lofty branches, there lived a cat by the name of Lomasa. Lomasa was the happiest of cats, for there was a never-ending supply of birds and other small creatures to eat, and he never went short of a meal.

One day, however, a man – an outcast – arrived in the forest. He built himself a hut and set traps throughout the area in order to

catch the creatures that lived there for his food and sport. Of course any wise animal knew to stay well clear, but one day Lomasa was overcome with temptation by the meat left in one of the traps and forgot to be wary, and suddenly the cat found himself caught fast in the snare. Lomasa pulled and tugged and tugged and pulled, but he couldn't free himself from the netting that held him captive.

The mouse, overjoyed to find his enemy incapacitated, ventured out to explore for himself, as he could do so now without fear of becoming the cat's next meal. Thus Palita roamed with impunity, growing so bold as to venture right up to the trap to sample the meat, and even climbing onto the cat himself.

Palita was wrong to be so confident, however, because the mouse was not as free from danger as he thought. Approaching quickly came a mongoose by the name of Harita. Detecting the tempting scent of the mouse, he had come to claim his prey.

That was not all; on a branch of the banyan tree was an owl, named Chandraka, known for his sharp beak. He too had spied the mouse, and was likewise intent upon making it his dinner. Danger lurked on every side now for Palita, with three creatures all wanting him for their own.

The mouse – who as we know, was very wise – didn't lose his head in terror at the situation he found himself in, and instead carefully considered his options. The mongoose, he knew, would be upon him the moment he left the trap. The owl, however, would pounce on him if he remained where he was. And if the cat were to free himself, then it would truly all be over for Palita.

Now again, considering his options, the mouse, swift of thought and wisdom, concluded that he could not ensure his own safety by himself, and that his best chance for survival was to team up with the enemy that was currently at the greatest disadvantage: the cat.

For the cat, thought the mouse, although an enemy, was in great distress. It would, therefore, be in the cat's best interests to listen to what he, Palita, had to say. All he had to do was convince the cat of this fact, and he could buy the cat's protection from the other two foes who waited to devour him.

So, Palita told the cat that he came in friendship and he proposed a deal. If the hunter returned and found the cat in the trap, Palita pointed out, then Lomasa would not live for long. He, the mouse, could gnaw through the netting to free the cat, but only if the cat promised to shelter him from the other two enemies in return.

The cat, seeing the sense in what the mouse said, agreed to the deal. Palita then moved to lie beneath Lomasa, safe and hidden from harm as he had intended. The mongoose and owl were amazed by this, and realized that they would not be able to get to the mouse without putting themselves in danger from the cat. Knowing that they were beaten, they each returned to their own homes.

The mouse, greatly relieved, felt his spirits lift considerably. The cat, however, was not so happy; now that his end of the bargain had been upheld, surely it was time for the mouse to deliver his and set him free? For although little Palita was working at the strings of the net as promised, he was working much more slowly than the fearful cat would have liked, and he soon grew impatient. Lomasa urged the mouse to go faster, worried that the hunter would soon return.

There was no need for more speed, the mouse assured him. It was always best to wait to begin something at the right time, not wasting time by doing so too early. If carried out at the right moment, then the results would be exactly as they both required.

But what was that perfect moment? Palita explained that he would wait to cut that final string until the moment the hunter appeared. Then, and only then, would he do so, because at that moment they would both be at their most terrified: the cat, of the hunter, and the mouse at the fact the cat was now free. The cat would be thinking only of fleeing to save his own life, and not of eating the mouse – and only then could they both be safe and free.

Lomasa was not happy with this, and argued his case for the mouse releasing him sooner. But Palita was resolute, countering each argument with one of his own. He would not be moved: no matter how greatly the cat professed undying devotion and friendship, he would not free him until he decided the time was right. There was no such thing as a friend or foe, Palita pointed out, only circumstances that creates one or the other – and when those circumstances changed, who could be certain that their alliance would remain?

The night passed, with the mouse sheltering beneath the still entangled cat. When morning came, Lomasa's terror soared, for, as he had feared, the hunter returned bearing weapons and accompanied by a pack of angry dogs. Only then did Palita, true to his word, nibble through the final string, setting the cat free. As the mouse had predicted, the cat bolted, running up the banyan to safety, while Palita too fled, darting back into his hole.

Safe now, the cat sought to continue his conversation with his rescuer. Why had the mouse run away so quickly, he asked, for surely they were friends now? Did he really think that he, Lomasa, would do him harm now after what they had been through together?

But the mouse would not be tempted: they had been allies out of expediency, and now that the moment of danger was past, Palita was not willing to put it to the test. Thus the mouse demonstrated an important message: sometimes it is necessary to make peace with a powerful enemy.

The Mystery of the Goddess Li Shou

A quick internet search for 'cat deities' will provide the reader with a wealth of information in this area.

One frequently mentioned deity is said to be the ancient Chinese goddess known as Li Shou. According to a popular and often cited story, Li Shou was originally put in charge of the earth. Unfortunately, true to her feline nature, Li Shou was far fonder of sleeping than being active, and spent a lot of the time dozing comfortably under a cherry tree while the world fell into disorder and chaos around her. Finally the other deities had enough and Li Shou was stripped of her role and humankind was put in charge of the earth instead.

Despite this less than glowing origin story, Li Shou is said to bring good luck and prosperity, as well as protecting crops by chasing away mice and other rodents that threaten to spoil them.

What is most interesting about the goddess however is the debate regarding whether or not she actually originated in China at all. Despite being frequently mentioned online, there is a distinct lack of sources for her in the writings of Classical China, and it has been suggested that Li Shou is actually a more modern invention from outside of Asia.

PART 2

Cats of Fairy Tale, Lore and Legend

As with every other area of our lives, cats have managed to firmly insert a paw or two into our stories and legends. Whether meek and mild, or cunning and curious, the cat is portrayed as friend or foe, supporter or adversary, and pretty much everything in between.

Some of these tales are well known, while others perhaps less so. Who was the cat said to have killed King Arthur? What do cats and vampires have in common? And just why are dogs and mice the life-long enemies of the cat?

While such stories often entertain and amuse, they also serve another purpose: helping us to better understand our feline companions, their relationships with others, and, ultimately, as so often with folklore, telling us more about ourselves.

Ferocious Felines

Folklore is filled with many strange and wonderful creatures: some dark and menacing, others intriguing and alluring. With their enigmatic behaviour, penchant for roaming the night and lurking in the shadows, cats have long been a popular focus of our tales and legends: whether these be stories of fearsome critters lurking in the lumber woods or terrifying vampire cats waiting to suck our blood, the cat is never far away.

Feline Fashion Police: The Yule Cat

Although generally a time of celebration, not all folklore surrounding the midwinter period is warm and cosy. Iceland is home to some of the most terrifying festive folklore around, and the *Jólakötturinn* or Yule Cat, is one particularly ferocious example.

This fearful creature is said to punish anyone who is not given new clothes at Christmas, attacking them and tearing them to shreds. It is highly recommended, therefore, to put new clothes at the top of your Christmas wish list!

Today the Yule Cat is a typical bogeyman-type character used to 'encourage' small children to behave themselves, especially in the run-up to Christmas, but the creature's origins are not entirely clear.

The poem 'Jólakötturinn' was published in the book *Jólin Koma*, or *Christmas is Coming*, by Jóhannes úr Kötlum in 1932. It is through these popular poems that many of Iceland's well-loved Christmas figures originated and passed into popular folklore. An English translation of *Jólin Koma* in 2015 brought Kötlum's work, and the Yule Cat with it, to an even wider audience.

Kötlum's inspiration was, in turn, the 19th-century Icelandic author Jón Árnason, famed for his collection of folktales first published in 1862. This is believed to be the first mention of the Yule Cat in print, and indeed some argue that there is no hard evidence for the existence of the Yule Cat before Árnason's work.

Another theory suggests that the Yule Cat didn't actually originate as a folkloric figure, but instead came about through a misunderstanding of a figure of speech. Árnason references a saying 'To dress the cat' – also 'to dress the Yule Cat' – recording that those who didn't receive new clothes for the festive season would 'dress the cat'. This essentially means that those who are not given new clothes for Christmas remain in the same clothes, just as a cat doesn't change what it wears. It has been posited, therefore, that Árnason misunderstood this phrase, thinking it referred to an actual folkloric creature – and thus the spectre of the Yule Cat was born.

Other ideas argue in favour of a much older provenance. One such theory is that the Yule Cat was spawned from a wider folkloric tradition in Scandinavian belief linked to that well-known forerunner to Father Christmas, St Nicholas. It was said that during midwinter the saint roamed the land distributing presents to children; attended by a demon, he was also responsible for punishing the bad and the naughty. It has been theorized that this demon was the origin of the Scandinavian Yule Goat, and the Yule Cat may have had a similar provenance. Goats weren't originally common in Iceland, and it is possible that, through misunderstanding or mistranslation, the original goat may have at some point morphed into a cat.

Although not appearing in the same poem, the Yule Cat quickly became connected with other festive creatures in the book, such as the troll Gryla and her 13 prankster children, the Yule Lads. The Yule Cat is now often seen as the feline pet of the Yule Lads, though this was never a connection made by Árnason or Kötlum. It is said that the smallest of the Yule Lads, Stúfur, rides the Yule Cat like a horse.

Whatever its origins, by the last quarter of the 20th century the Yule Cat was fully entrenched in Iceland's Christmas traditions. This reach was further enhanced in 1987 when popular Icelandic singer Björk released her song 'Jólakötturinn'. Adpating Kötlum's poem into song form, it describes how the Yule Cat prowls the festive countryside looking for children who have not received new clothes to devour.

In November 2018, a 5m (16½ft) iron sculpture of the Yule Cat was erected in the centre of Reykjavík. This provoked a mixed reaction: covered with lights, and costing the city approximately 4.4 million Icelandic króna, – approximately $36,000 or £25,954 pounds sterling – it was seen as a somewhat tone-deaf use of public funds during the cost-of-living crisis at the time.

Be Careful Where You Look: The Skoffín

Another terrifying feline creature from Iceland is the Skoffín. Said to be the result of a male arctic fox mating with a she-cat, in appearance it resembles a cross between these two animals, and it is said to be completely deadly.

The Skoffín's gaze is believed to instantly kill anything in its path, and, like many other such creatures, the Skoffín is notoriously difficult to defeat. Among the limited options available, only silver bullets are said to be effective in killing a Skoffín or, at a pinch, a silver button with a cross on it might work. The deadly gaze of the Skoffín, its greatest weapon, can also be used against itself, and the surest way to kill one was said to be either by its own reflection or the gaze of another Skoffín.

According to one popular tale, a particularly nasty Skoffín lay in wait one day for a church service to finish. The congregation, completely unaware of the danger awaiting them, left the building – each one falling down dead the second they crossed the threshold. The priest, thankfully a clever and resourceful man, realized quickly what was happening, and told the rest of the congregation to stay inside. He then took a mirror and slid it out of the door. The Skoffín, faced with his own reflection, died instantly and the remaining people were saved.

It is said that, unlike kittens, Skoffín young are born with their eyes already open. If not killed immediately, they will sink down into the ground where they are unreachable; there they will remain for three years before emerging as fully mature and deadly adult Skoffín.

It is possible that, over time, Skoffín-lore has been conflated with or confused with that of the basilisk, and indeed it is thought by some to be an Icelandic version of this legendary creature. The basilisk was also said to be able to kill with its gaze, and could be destroyed by its own reflection.

Another origin story about the Skoffín states that – in a similar way to the cockatrice – the creature is the result of the impossible event of a rooster laying an egg. This only occurs when a rooster lives to an extremely old age, and the egg can be distinguished from a hen's egg by its much smaller size. If such an egg is allowed to hatch, then a Skoffín is born.

Beware the Wampus Cat

A popular legend in the Appalachian region of the eastern United States and elsewhere is that of the Wampus Cat. This creature is known by various names from area to area – including the Whistling Wampus in Arkansas and the Gallywampus in Missouri – and it is said to terrify anyone who sees it.

Descriptions of the Wampus Cat vary, but it is generally said to be half-cat, half-dog in appearance. Some say that it resembles a cross between a panther and a pit bull dog, while others describe it as more hyena-like, or even a cross between a mountain lion and a human woman. The Wampus Cat might run on all fours, but has also been described as moving upright on two legs.

Emanating evil, the Wampus has yellow, haunting eyes that glow in the dark and sharp fangs and claws, and its screams can be heard for miles around. It is a beast best avoided, as it is said to lurk in the shadows, waiting to pounce on the unsuspecting; those who see it run the risk of being driven insane. When it comes to prey, according to some sources the Wampus Cat has a preference for eagles. It is said to mimic the sound of mountain goats in order to try and trick the majestic birds into swooping lower, making them easier to pick off.

The Wampus Cat is reputedly notoriously hard to kill: the female of the species can only be killed with a crosscut saw, while the males are almost impossible to defeat. According to one somewhat tongue-in-cheek source, there is only one creature known for certain to be able to bring down the Wampus: the Whiffenpoofit that comes down both sides of the river at once and so confuses the Wampus Cat that it vanishes. Furthermore, Wampus footprints are impossible to track, as they only show up on solid rock.

Said to appear at twilight or dawn, like many a good urban legend, the Wampus Cat has been used to strike fear into the hearts of children as a cautionary tale. Whether to stop them from straying away from safety, or as a reminder to be home before dark, the spectre of the Wampus Cat is also particularly popular at summer camps in the USA as a way to keep large groups of children in line.

One of the earliest traceable records of the Wampus Cat in the historical record is from the *Greenville Sun* for 17 December 1918, where it stated that the creature, known for generations, had again been seen roaming the area. The Wampus is listed as 'an undefined imaginary animal' in a later source, and it is also mentioned in Henry Tryon's 1939 collection of lumberjack folklore, *Fearsome Critters*. According to Tryon, the Wampus Cat caused many problems in the lumber camps, including scaring away all available game apart from the 'fool hen', and stopping fish from biting for seven days after it passed through a stream.

Purported sightings of the Wampus over the years have further fuelled belief in its existence. Many people claim to have seen or heard the fearsome creature, while some even say they have been attacked by it. Wampus Cat, in keeping with other such cryptids, has also been blamed for the death of livestock and dogs on numerous occasions, including an incident in Quitman, Mississippi, in 1913 where the corpses of 102 dogs were discovered after flooding, stripped of flesh and fur.

One possible origin for the Wampus legend is the misidentification of panthers or bobcats, while some speculate that the Wampus Cat might actually be a species previously thought to be extinct.

That the Wampus Cat has captured the popular imagination is reflected in the term passing into common usage: declaring something is 'catty wampus' is a popular saying in some parts of the USA, meaning that something is mixed up or out of the usual order of things. It can also be used to refer to something that is crooked or uneven. Again reflecting its popularity, several high schools across the United States have the Wampus Cat as their mascot, including schools in Texas, Arkansas, Oklahoma, Louisiana, Idaho and North Carolina.

It is believed that, originally, the Wampus legend has links to the folklore of the Tsalagi (Cherokee People). It is now, however, better known as a general urban legend or tall tale, far removed from these roots.

Vampire Cats

Night-roaming, bloodthirsty, in search of their next victim – this description refers not to the much-maligned feline, but to that popular staple of folklore and legend: the vampire. Due to such similarities, however, the cat and this blood-sucking creature have, in some cultures, become inextricably linked.

One widespread belief is that cats are instrumental in turning people – particularly those already dead – into vampires. In China, cats are not allowed to enter a room that contains the dead: it is believed that if the cat leaps over the body then the corpse will turn into a vampire. In areas of Greece and North Macedonia, before burial the dead were watched all night long to make sure a cat or other creature did not jump over them as it was believed they would become a vampire. If the worst did happen, it was possible to undo the damage before transformation could occur: the corpse must be pierced with two long 'sack needles' to prevent them coming back, a belief that is akin to popular ideas about staking vampires. In Romania, it was believed that if a black cat crossed the path of a woman while she was pregnant, the child would become a vampire.

Then there is the belief that cats are vampires themselves. Vampire-lore often states that they have the ability to shapeshift, and the image of a vampire turning into a bat is particularly iconic. It might be surprising, therefore, to discover that in Slavic folklore cats are actually the vampire's animal of choice. Another shapeshifter is said to be Lilith, the first wife of the biblical Adam. It has been suggested that the myth of the vampire first arose from tales of Lilith shifting into cat form, and there is a later idea that, in the form of a fierce cat creature named El Broosha, she sucked the blood from sleeping infants.

The Tlahuelpuchi, a bloodsucking creature from the folklore of Tlaxcala, Mexico, is a type of vampire-witch. Born with this curse, the Tlahuelpuchi tends to feed on children, draining their blood at night, and bruises on the upper body of a dead child or other victim were said to be evidence that the Tlahuelpuchi was responsible. The creature's favourite time to strike was said to be around 4am, when unsuspecting victims and families were asleep. If the intended target was a long distance away, the Tlahuelpuchi transformed into a bird to fly there, but if the victim was nearer, it would walk in the form of animal such as a cat, dog or coyote. It then transformed into a turkey – its preferred form – when it reached its destination, before carrying out its bloody task.

In the historical region of Bengal, in the north-east of India, there was a creature known to the Kurukh or Oraon peoples as the Chordewa. A form of vampire-witch, the Chordewa was said to transform its soul into the form of a black cat, and, in this guise, gain entry into a household in order to prey on the sick and dying. Although the Chordewa looked like a normal cat, there was a clue for those who knew what to look for: the Chordewa had a distinctive miaow that betrayed its true identity. Once inside, the Chordewa would jump onto the bed of the sick person and eat their food. It would then go to lick the lips of the dying person – if the Chordewa was successful the person was doomed to die.

The Vampire Cat of Nabéshima

Belief in the vampiric nature of cats can also be found in Japan. The tale of 'The Vampire Cat of Nabéshima' in *Tales of Old Japan*, published in 1871 by British diplomat and writer Algernon Freeman-Mitford, is one such story. This collection of stories brought the idea of the vampire cat and other folkloric creatures to a wider audience outside of Japan.

The Prince of Hizen enjoyed the company of a woman who lived in his household by the name of O Toyo. She was of great beauty and intelligence, and a favourite of the prince. One evening they were returning to the palace after a day enjoying the beautiful grounds when – unseen by the couple – a black cat followed them inside.

They parted company, and O Toyo went to her room and settled to sleep. She awoke around midnight, to find a huge, terrifying cat watching her from the shadows. O Toyo cried out, but the cat leapt at her, killing her by digging its claws into her throat and cutting off her breath. The murderous feline buried her body in a shallow grave under the verandah, before transforming itself into the form of the murdered woman.

Blissfully unaware that his favourite had met with such a terrible fate, the prince continued to spend time with O Toyo as before, little realizing that he was being bewitched by the terrible creature. The prince began to suffer, his strength decreasing with each passing day, his face pale, and all signs pointing to a terrible sickness. In truth, O Toyo, or rather the creature that had taken her form, was nightly sucking the very life-blood from him.

The prince's household was very concerned, their alarm growing day by day. The greatest physicians were called, but none could determine what ailed the steadily worsening prince. The only clue they had was that the prince seemed to suffer most greatly at night time. It was decided by the prince's councillors that a guard of 100 of the palace retainers would stand outside the prince's room each night to try and find out what ailed him.

This seemed a good plan, but unfortunately they had not reckoned on the bewitchment of O Toyo. Each night, as it drew near to 10pm, one by one the guards would find themselves overcome with drowsiness and the overwhelming need to sleep. And so, come midnight, when O Toyo came to the prince, there was no one awake to witness her draining the prince of more of his life force.

Utterly perplexed, three of the prince's chief councillors decided to stay awake and see for themselves, only to find that they were overtaken by sleep just like the guards. After this, they discussed the matter and came to a conclusion: the prince was being bewitched.

With this decided, they called upon Ruiten, the chief priest at the temple, asking him to come to the palace to pray for the prince with the hope of bringing some relief. Ruiten came to the palace and did so, though the prince continued to decline. One night at around midnight, awake and praying in his rooms for the health of the prince, Ruiten heard a noise outside. Peering out, he saw a soldier washing in the well down below, before praying to the figure of Buddha there for the prince to recover his health and well-being.

Impressed with his dedication, the priest called to him, and the man revealed his identity as Ito Soda. He was a lowly soldier, not worthy of gaining access to the prince, but he wanted nothing more than to help his prince be well. What is more, Ito Soda believed that he would be able to help if he were allowed to spend just one night with the men who guarded him.

Ruiten, even more impressed with Soda's dedication, arranged for this to happen, and so Ito Soda settled with the guard that night. Sure enough, as it reached 10 o'clock, one by one the guards started to succumb to overwhelming tiredness. Not Ito Soda, however; he had come prepared, and, after spreading oil paper over the mats in order that they would not be defiled, took out a small knife that he had brought with him. Feeling the increasing need to sleep, he stuck the blade into his own thigh, the pain keeping him wide awake.

This worked for a time, but then he again felt sleep trying to claim him. Not to be outdone, the faithful soldier reached for the handle of the knife, twisting it into the wound and sparking fresh agony. It was in this way that he managed to stay awake, and he was rewarded around midnight when he saw the sliding doors to the prince's rooms slowly open and a beautiful woman enter. She smiled to see the sleeping guards, but her expression turned to a frown when she spied Ito Soda, still clearly awake. She had not seen him before: who was he, and what was he doing? The man explained his purpose and how he was managing to keep himself awake. O Toyo hid her displeasure as best she could, and stayed by the prince for some time, but each time she tried to get close enough to work her spells on the prince, Ito Soda glared at her and she was unable to continue her evil endeavours. Frustrated, she finally left, returning to her rooms, and the prince slept peacefully through the night.

Ito Soda reported what had occurred to the head councillor the following morning, and they agreed that he should keep watch the next night as well in order to determine what was going on. O Toyo appeared at the same time once again, but, seeing that Ito Soda was awake, she went back to her own rooms. And so it was that the prince, no longer molested during his sleeping hours, started to grow well again, colour returning to his cheeks and his health vastly improving. It was also noted that the guards no longer experienced the strange sleepiness each night now that O Toyo did not visit, a connection that was not missed by Ito Soda, who related this coincidence to the councillors. He also expressed his suspicion that O Toyo was not in fact a mortal woman at all, but some creature or goblin who had bewitched the prince.

How could they kill it, they wanted to know. Again, Ito Soda had the answer: he would go to her room and attempt to kill her, but, if she managed to escape, the chief advisor and eight of his best men should be waiting outside ready to shoot her. And so Soda went to O Toyo's rooms under the pretext of delivering a letter. When he attacked her, she reached for a halberd and the two fought with their blades. Realizing that Ito Soda was going to beat her, in desperation O Toyo transformed into her true form, and he found himself face to face with the monstrous cat. Taking advantage of his surprise, the cat leapt for the roof, and, despite the men outside, made good her escape.

The cat took up refuge in the mountains, and became a well-known menace to the people who lived nearby. Finally, fully restored to health, the prince ordered a hunting party to track down the cat and kill it; they were successful, and the terrible creature was no more.

The prince did not forget his faithful servant, and Ito Soda was promoted and rewarded for his loyalty.

Alien Big Cats of Britain

Particularly prominent in Britain over the last fifty years or so are sightings of mysterious, unidentified, large cats. Often likened to pumas, panthers, leopards or lynxes in appearance, these purported sightings have sparked intense interest and debate.

Among the most high-profile cases in England is the Beast of Bodmin Moor in Cornwall. Said to be a black or dark coloured large cat, sightings began in the late 1970s and the beast has been witnessed on numerous occasions since. In 1995 an official investigation into sightings of the Beast was launched by the British Government, but no firm evidence of its existence was discovered.

Another famous 'alien cat' can be found in Exmoor National Park in Devon and Somerset. The Beast of Exmoor is said to be similar to a puma or panther in appearance, with witnesses putting the Beast at between 1m and 2m (3–6½ ft) in length, from nose to tail tip.

But what is behind such sightings? Theories include the intentional release or accidental escape of animals from private collections, zoos or wildlife sanctuaries, or the misidentification of common wild or domesticated animals. Then there are more outlandish ideas such as the suggestion that these 'cats' are not actually physical beings at all, but are a thought projection. Finally is the idea that they are exactly what they seem to be – unidentified large cats native to Britain that have somehow gone undiscovered.

Although proliferating in modern times, the idea of large unexplained felines – sometimes blamed for unexpected livestock deaths in an area – is not without precedence. William Cobbett, the famous 18th-century pamphleteer, politician and farmer from Farnham, Surrey, recounted a strange sight he had witnessed as a young boy. By a hollow elm tree near Waverley Abbey, he had seen a 'big grey cat, as big as a middle-sized spaniel dog'. Looking back on the incident many years later, Cobbett opined that it was similar to a 'great wild grey cat' that he had seen in New Brunswick, Canada. Despite being ridiculed for the admission, he refused to withdraw his assertion.

The Fairy Cat: Cat Sìth

The creature known primarily in Scottish folklore as the Cat Sìth or Cait Sidhe in Irish, is said to be a type of fairy that appears as a terrifying large black cat with a white spot on its chest.

The name literally translates as 'fairy cat', and the creature was generally seen as a malevolent being. One belief surrounding the Cat Sìth was that it had the power to steal someone's soul after death before it could reach God. As a result, practices were put in place to stop this happening: special wakes known as the Late Wake or *fèill fhadalach* were held to keep the creature away from a corpse before burial could take place, and loud music and general noise were created to scare the Cat Sìth away. In some areas it was said that at Samhain the Cat Sìth would bless houses with a saucer of milk outside, and curse those without. Some believed that the Cat Sìth was a witch and could turn into a cat nine times – on the ninth time, it would be stuck in that form.

The Cat Sìth – like most cats – was said to be attracted by the warmth of a fire, and so it was forbidden to light a fire in the same room as the dead for fear the creature would appear.

It has been suggested that the idea of the Cat Sìth originated from European wildcats, or the Scottish wildcat-domestic cat hybrid, the Kellas cat.

King Arthur's Killer: The Cath Palug

The great deeds of the heroic King Arthur and his Knights of the Round Table are some of the most well-known legends in our shared history, familiar across the globe. They are often among the first adventure stories that children hear, captivated by tales of valiant battles and the iconic pulling of the sword from the stone. Some even say that King Arthur and his knights sleep beneath a hill or mountain, waiting for the moment when the kingdom needs them most, at which time they will awaken to save humankind from the greatest of perils.

But did you know that in some stories the famed King Arthur meets a gruesome end at the claws of a cat? The creature, known variously as Cath Palug, Cath Baluc or Cath Paluc, and whose name means 'to dig, wound, scratch, claw or pierce' – literally the 'scratching cat' – has been associated with Arthur since around the 11th century CE.

Monster cats in general were popular in Irish folklore, and it is likely that the Cath Palug has links and origins among other sea cat creatures of Irish tradition. There is a description of one such creature in the 8th- or early 9th-century Irish epic the *Navigatio sancti Brendani abbatis – Voyage of St Brendan the*

Abbot: 'There is a great sea-cat here like a young ox or a three year old horse, overgrown by feeding on the fish of this sea and this island.' The monster swims in pursuit of the saint's boat: 'Bigger than a brazen cauldron was each of his eyes: a boar's tusks had he: fuzzy hair upon him; and he had the maw of a leopard with the strength of a lion, and the voracity of a hound.'

The first known reference to a connection between the Cath Palug and King Arthur or his knights is the 10th-century poem 'Pa Gur yv y Porthaur' ('Who is the Porter?') in the *Llyfr Du Caerfyrddin* (*The Black Book of Carmarthen*). Believed to date from around the last quarter of the 12th century, *The Black Book* tells how Cai or Kay – one of Arthur's greatest warriors – battled against the Cath Palug in Ynys Môn (Anglesey). During the encounter, nine score – 180 – warriors were killed by the creature, and Kay's shield was 'polished' against Cath Palug.

Another reference appears in the 13th-century *Three Powerful Swineherds* triad of *The Triads of the Island of Britain*. It is here that the origin of the creature is explained: a kitten was born to the great white sow called Henwen at the black rock in Llanfair, Arfon. It was cast into the sea by the swineherd, but the sons of Palug in Anglesey rescued it and nurtured and protected the cat, little knowing that it was to become one of the three great plagues on the island.

In the French Arthurian romances of the late 12th and 13th centuries, there are mentions of a creature known as Le Cap Alu or Capalu. To the French, Cath Palug was, quite literally, 'the bog cat'. A fight is alluded to, in which Arthur slays – or is slain by – a cat monster.

Versions of the story where Arthur meets his death at the claws of the Cath Palug are generally thought to have been attempts by French authors to mock the English, with passages such as: 'King Arthur was pushed by Capalu into the bog; and the cat killed him in war, then passed over to England and was not slow to conquer it – then wore the crown in the land and was the lord of the country.' In another French variant, Capalu abducts Arthur and takes him away to the magical island of Avalon, his final resting place.

The *Estoire de Merlin* or *The Story of Merlin*, a 13th-century French prose romance, mentions Arthur's victorious engagement against a monster cat. The fight is said to take place near the Lac du Bourget, Savoy, France. From the 14th century onwards, this location was known as Mont du Chat, hinting at the link to the Arthurian legend.

According to this source, a fisherman comes to the Lac de Lausanne with his nets. 'He vowed to give to God the first fish he should take, but he breaks his vow three times. The third time he cast in his net he drew out a kitten; he nourished it, and it strangled him and his wife, and children, and fled to the mountain and destroyed all it saw.'

Hearing of this terrible creature, Arthur commands his men to ride with him to track it down. The cat leaps from the cave and rushes at Arthur, and when Arthur tries to pierce it with his spear, the cat breaks it in his mouth. Arthur then smites the cat on its head, but the creature retaliates, grabbing the king and drawing blood. Refusing to be bested, Arthur runs at the cat, holding his shield before him: the cat's claws get stuck in the shield and it is unable to free itself. While it is incapacitated, Arthur cuts off its forelegs, but the cat manages to attack once more, aiming for Arthur's throat. It bites him, and, with blood gushing from his neck, Arthur cuts off its hind feet, slaying the creature once and for all as it tries to escape to its cave.

Arthur survives, tended to by Merlin and his men. Before returning to Gaul, Arthur asks what the mountain is called, and says that from henceforth it shall be known as the Mountain of the Cat.

It is highly likely that, on etymological grounds, the Capalu or Chapalu of the French romances comes from the Old Welsh Cath Palug, suggesting therefore that *The Black Book* and the Welsh sources are the earliest sources for this fearsome creature.

References to Arthur and his connection with the cat exist not only in literary form. At the start of the 12th century, an Arthurian legend was carved on the *Porta della Pescheria* – the Fish Market Door – of Modena Cathedral, near Bologna in Italy, a popular stopping point for pilgrims making the journey to Rome.

Another artistic rendition of Arthur's involvement with the Cath Palug can be found in south-east Italy at Otranto Cathedral. In 1165 the Archbishop of Otranto commissioned an enormous mosaic, and the king is depicted in one of the scenes. Arthur – identified as *Rex Arturus* – is seen sitting astride a goat and battling against a large cat, with a caption reading: 'The demon Cath Palug from the Welsh Tradition'.

There is another suggestion regarding the origin of the Cath Palug. The 13th-century French epic poem *La Bataille Loquifer* (*The Battle of Loquifer*) describes the monster as having the 'head of a cat, feet of a dragon, body of a horse,' and the 'queue of a lion,' suggesting that Cath Palug was perhaps a Chimera-type creature.

Ghost of the Capitol: Demon Cat

The Capitol Building has been a central landmark in Washington, DC, USA, for over 200 years. The meeting place of Congress – the legislative branch of the US government – since 1800, the building has another claim to fame: it is said to be home to a variety of ghosts.

From revolutionary soldiers to former government officials, one of the Capitol's most famous spooks is known as Demon Cat. With the tongue-in-cheek nickname of 'DC', this spectral feline dates back to the mid-19th century, and continues to fascinate and terrify visitors to this day.

According to legend, Demon Cat appears, on first sight, to be nothing extraordinary: just a regular-sized cat. But appearances can be deceiving; as it draws closer, the creature grows rapidly, reaching gigantic proportions before the terrified onlooker invariably passes out from sheer terror.

The first written references to Demon Cat date from the late 19th century, with a story of a night watchman who was attacked by a cat that grew to the size of an elephant as he looked on in horror. An article in *The Washington Post*, 2 October 1898, 'Spooks of the Capitol: The Specters That Haunt the Houses of Congress', appears to be the earliest

written record of the legend, where it describes how the cat was shot at by a guard in 1892, and hadn't, at that point, been seen since. Over the years that followed, the original stories were embellished by word of mouth and further discussion in the press, with additional details such as the guard dying of a heart attack brought on by his terrifying encounter.

The appearance of Demon Cat has taken on mythic proportions, and the spectre is said to have presaged a number of disasters in US history, including sightings before the assassinations of Abraham Lincoln and John F Kennedy, and before the stock market crash of 1929.

Although the idea of a monstrous, ghostly cat is infinitely more exciting, one potential origin for the legend is rather more mundane. Cats were a familiar sight in the basement of the Capitol building, introduced to help keep rats and mice in check. Consequently, it has been suggested that night watchmen may have misinterpreted what they were seeing in the dark, leading to the advent of the legend. Architectural factors could also have played a part, with the design of the building lending itself to acoustics perfect for amplifying the sound of caterwauling from the resident mouse-hunters.

Modern-day visitors who tour the Capitol hoping for a glimpse of the spectral feline have so far been out of luck – the last reported appearance of Demon Cat is said to have been in 1963. For those hoping for a glimpse, however, Demon Cat is rumoured to frequent the Whispering Gallery, an acoustically designed chamber where a whisper spoken in one part of the room can be heard clearly on the opposite side, and the crypt, a large, circular room located beneath the Capitol Rotunda.

For those sceptical of the cat's existence, there is physical evidence that helps keep the legend alive; half a dozen paw prints set into the floor at the base of a column in the Small Senate Rotunda are said to be 'concrete' proof that Demon Cat exists.

Japan's Supernatural Cats

In Japan there is a strong belief in the supernatural, and *yōkai* is the name given to a whole host of creatures and spirits. Supernatural cats - or *kaibyo* as they are known - are one of the most popular, and there are many tales about them throughout Japan's history.

Such beliefs were particularly strong during the Edo period (1603-1868 CE), and it was during this time that tales of these supernatural cats developed into the legends we know today. One popular idea was that a domestic cat would become a *kaibyo* once it had lived to a certain age; it is said that people were so terrified of this that a cat would be killed when it reached the age of seven years to stop this from happening.

Nekomata

The yōkai known as nekomata is one of Japan's oldest and most well-known supernatural cats, dating from the Kamakura period (1185–1333). Sources talk of a terrifying creature that dwelt in the mountains, preying on people who ventured too far into the forests.

One of the earliest references comes from the 13th century, when on 8 August 1233 a creature with 'eyes like a cat and a body the size of a great dog' was said to have devoured several people in the mountains in Nanto-shi, a city in modern-day Toyama prefecture, Japan. In accounts of the nekomata from this time there is nothing supernatural about the creature; it is clearly perceived as an all-too-real physical threat lurking in the mountains, a wild beast ready to attack and devour the unsuspecting.

Theories for the origin of the belief in nekomata include sightings of actual escaped lions or tigers, rabid dogs, and they have even been suggested as evidence of the yamanelev – a prehistoric mountain lion.

It was during the Edo Period – the golden age of the Japanese yōkai – that the nekomata began to take on the more recognizable supernatural form familiar today. Instead of being a distinct type of wild cat lurking in the mountains, the nekomata was now said to have been a normal house cat.

Upon reaching a certain age, its tail split and it transformed into a nekomata, before heading to the mountains to live out its life in this form.

During this time, descriptions of the nekomata also underwent a significant change: originally said to be the size of a large dog, a source from 1685 records it as larger than a wild boar, and in 1775 a nekomata was described as the size of a panther or lion. By the early 19th century it had grown even more, with an account from 1809 stating that the creature was over 1.8m (6ft), long and capable of carrying off fully grown dogs with ease.

Largely instrumental in the development of the nekomata legend was Sadatake Ise's *Ansai Zuihitsu*, which states that: 'A cat that is several years of age will come to have two tails, and become the yōkai called nekomata.' The idea and image was then spread to a wider audience by the scholar Arai Hakuseki, who included the idea of the split-tailed nekomata in his collection of essays on cat-themed mysteries.

The mountain-dwelling nature of the nekomata and its origins are preserved in the names of places associated with historical nekomata attacks, including Nekomata Mountain in Toyama prefecture, and Nekomata Peak, Fukushima.

Today, nekomata are a far cry from the fearsome creatures they used to represent: like many yōkai, they are now generally portrayed in a cartoonish, cute fashion.

The Kasha

The demon known as the kasha, famed for its penchant for devouring corpses, is today perceived in the form of a terrifying, flaming cat.

Originally, however, the kasha had no link to cats at all: it was originally said to be a burning cart drawn by devils or demons that came down from the sky to steal coffins or corpses during a funeral.

During the Kamakura period, Hell Scrolls or jigoku-zoshi became popular, depicting in graphic detail the suffering and pain that awaited the dead at the hands of the dreaded oni – terrible demons – that would flay the skin from their bones. These scrolls included depictions of the oni transporting their victims on flaming carts – which evolved into the idea that the oni collected sinners on their carts to take them away for torture and judgement.

With the advent of the Edo period, however, the oni were no longer associated with the kasha: instead, the cart was an entity all on its own, coming down from the sky in high winds and thunder to collect the dead. It was believed that if thunder was heard overhead during a funeral, then the dreaded kasha was coming.

It was not until later in the Edo period in depictions of the kasha by artist Toriyama Sekien in his *The Illustrated Night*

Parade of a Hundred Demons (1776) that the kasha became primarily identified as a cat. Known for adding his own interpretations onto folkloric creatures and ideas, Sekien depicted the kasha as a flaming cat demon: this idea took hold and became the standard image of a kasha.

The *Bōsō Manroku* (1833), written by Chihara Kyosai, relates how a thunderstorm occurred during a funeral procession and high winds whisked the coffin up into the skies. A kasha descended to claim the body, in the form of a fierce, flesh-eating cat spirit.

Hokuetsu Seppu (1837) by Suzuki Bokushi, includes a story ascribed to the Tensho era (1573–92) involving another interrupted funeral. This time, a gust of wind and a vast fireball containing a huge, split-tailed cat are the culprits. The cat snatches up the coffin, but a quick-thinking priest beats it away with his staff.

The kasha was greatly feared, and it became taboo to leave a cat in the same room or even the same house as the dead, with any cat being banished upon a death. It also became common to weigh down a coffin in order to prevent it being stolen away by the kasha.

Another belief developed where it was actually the presence of the dead themselves that caused a cat to transform into a kasha: the kasha would then steal the body.

There are clear similarities between belief surrounding nekomata and kasha. It is sometimes said that kasha were, like nekomata, pets that had changed form upon reaching a certain age. Nekomata, in turn, have sometimes been depicted with fireballs hovering over their tails, with obvious kasha connotations. Both were also said to be able to raise the dead by leaping over a coffin.

Bakeneko

The last of the three main types of supernatural cat from Japan is the bakeneko. This yōkai, whose name means 'changed cat', is often confused or conflated with the nekomata, and there are several similarities between their legends.

As with the nekomata, it was said that a cat would transform into a bakeneko upon living a certain number of years. This number varied from location to location, but variously 7, 12 or 13 years were said to be when this transformation would take place.

Bakeneko had a variety of decidedly dangerous skills attributed to them: according to legend they were known to curse and possess people, speak using human language, manipulate the dead and shapeshift into human form.

The bakeneko was said to be particularly fond of lamp oil, and finding a cat licking oil from a lamp was believed to be a good way of identifying one of these terrifying supernatural fiends. There was a more logical explanation for a cat's love of lamp oil, however: during the Edo period, when tales of the bakeneko were particularly rife, lamps were lit using cheap fish oils. Cats – as obligate carnivores with limited protein sources due to the traditional human diet of grains and pulses of the time – would lick the fish oil from the lamps in order to try to address this deficiency.

Cats and their Tails

Along with their ears and whiskers, the tail – which plays a vital role in balance and communication – is perhaps the most readily identifiable feature of a cat. Coming in great variations in length, thickness and texture, it is through the movements of a cat's tail that it is possible to gauge how they are feeling and, to a foe, whether they are about to strike.

This highly important appendage features in a variety of different stories, legends and superstitions, and there is a wealth of folklore regarding cats and their tails.

The Tail of the Manx Cat

Along with ears and whiskers, a cat's tail is probably its most noted characteristic. Usually long and expressive, some cats have a tail that is truncated or even non-existent; this can be through accident or illness, or for reasons of genetics, a cat may be tailless from birth.

Across the globe, there are certain breeds of cat known for their shortened or missing tails, and one of the best known of these is the Manx cat. Originating on the Isle of Man, situated between north-west England and Northern Ireland, the tailless Manx cat has captured the popular imagination for centuries and, due to the breed's popularity, can now be found across the globe.

Although famed as the home of the Manx cat, originally the Isle of Man didn't have a native cat population at all. It is likely that cats first arrived on the island around the late 8th century CE, although the exact date is not known.

Known in Manx as *kayt Vanninagh* (singular) or *kiyt Vanninagh* (plural), the first reference to the Manx cat being tailless was in the 18th century, around 1730–50, when the term 'stubbin' was recorded. This was used to differentiate certain cats from the more common tailed variety, which is a strong indicator that there had been cats with truncated tails for long enough and in sufficient numbers that a specific name was needed for them.

There have been various ideas rooted in both science and genetics to try and explain the Manx's lack of tail. In *The Cat* (1881), biologist St George Jackson Mivart related how a female cat had its tail run over by the wheel of a cart; it was so damaged that it had to be cut off completely. The cat went on to have two litters of kittens; while the majority of the kittens were born with tails of the usual length, there were one or two that had small, stumpy, tails: this was – erroneously – taken as evidence that such traits could be hereditary.

There are many origin stories found in folklore to explain the Manx cat's missing tail. Several of these hold that the Manx has been lacking a tail since the days of Noah and the Great Flood:

Once upon a time, the Manx cat had a large, splendid tail. The cat was very proud of it and frequently showed off this fine attribute. How the Manx cat strutted and preened its way around the Ark, waving that tail for all to see. The cat in particular liked to taunt the dogs on board, walking slowly and extravagantly past its canine foes. The cat liked to tease and taunt the dogs so much that Noah had his work cut out, forever breaking up arguments and fights in an effort to protect the cat when the dogs inevitably had enough and went after it. After 40 days and 40 nights of such disturbance, Noah became quite frazzled!

At last, with a resounding jolt that reverberated throughout the vessel, the Ark found its resting place. Noah was now busier than ever, and his attention was directed towards more important matters than making sure the cat behaved. Seizing the opportunity, one of the dogs flew at the

cat, intent on getting its own back. Before anyone could intervene, the dog bit the cat's tail clean off.

How the cat yowled and screamed! But the damage was done. And the Manx cat has been without a tail ever since.

Another story takes place before the Manx cat even boarded the Ark. Known for living life on the edge, the Manx cat was nowhere to be seen when Noah called the animals to board the Ark. The other creatures, making their way in a timely fashion, were soon safely on board, but the cat dawdled as if there was all the time in the world.

Finally, Noah could wait no longer. As the Manx cat reached the Ark, the doors were closing. Shaken at last from its complacency, the cat began to run and leapt onto the Ark to reach safety. The cat succeeded, but alas! As the door slammed shut, the cat's tail was caught – it snapped clean off and fell into the water and was swept away.

Another story with biblical connections regarding the Manx cat involves judge and warrior Samson. According to this tale, Samson, always looking for ways to prove his strength, rejected the challenge of swimming the English Channel between France and England on the grounds that it was too easy a task. The Isle of Man, on the other hand, was a far more worthy test of his abilities, and so off he set. The journey was far harder than he had anticipated, however, and even this herculean hero started to struggle.

Growing wearier with each stroke, Samson battled on: finally he sighted land and the end was nearly in sight. But then calamity struck – for what should appear but a cat!

Without warning, the feline leapt onto his head. The weight dragged Samson down. In very real danger of drowning, he reached up and grabbed the creature by the tail, casting the cat into the sea. In his desperation, he had forgotten his own strength, and had torn the animal's tail off.

Another legend of the Manx cat harks back to the Spanish Armada of 1588. According to this story, a ship, part of the Spanish fleet, happened to be carrying tailless cats on board to deal with the mice and other vermin that would attack vital supplies during the voyage. This ship came to grief off the coast of the Isle of Man, but the cats, happily, survived, swimming their way to shore and safety. They settled on the island, and thus became the ancestors of the Manx cats we know today.

To commemorate this momentous event in the history of the island, the part of the coast where the ship is said to have been wrecked – the south-west tip of the island – is named Spanish Head. The fact that the fate of all ships from the Armada is known, and there is no record of one being wrecked off or near the Isle of Man, or the lack of tailless cats in Spain for that matter, can be glossed over for the sake of a good story.

Another potential shipwreck origin story was recorded in 1832 by English geologist and Anglican clergyman W B Clarke. Clarke wrote that while on holiday on the Isle of Man, he was told by someone in Castle Rushen that 'many years ago' a ship from Prussia or somewhere else in the Baltic had been wrecked between Castle Rushen and the Calf of Man off the south-west coast. A couple of tailless cats escaped and were caught by the wreckers, and it was from this pair that the rest of the Manx cat population originated.

It has also been said that, long ago, soldiers on the Isle of Man used to kill newborn cats in great numbers for their tails, which were cut off and stuck to shields and helmets as talismans during battle. This caused the she-cats of the island great sorrow, and they came up with a drastic solution to spare the lives of their kittens. When they were born, their mothers would bite off each kitten's tail, so that they could not be killed for it. After several generations of this practice, kittens started to be born without tails, and this is how the Manx cat came to appear as we know it today.

A more recent legend attributes the Manx cat's lack of tail to an unfortunate encounter when a motorcycle from the Isle of Man's TT (Tourist Trophy) race course ran over the tail of an over-confident cat.

There are various superstitions regarding the Manx cat. It was considered the height of bad luck to meet one on New Year's Day; all the more so if the encounter took place before an individual had seen the first footer or *quaaltagh* ('someone who meets') – the first person to enter the house after midnight who was said to herald the start of the new year.

It was also believed that the Manx cats had their own king. This regal feline was a normal cat by all appearances during the day, but, at night, it turned into a cat of fire, or rode in a carriage of fire. Beware, therefore, how you treat a Manx cat during the day, as at night it is said that the king remembers the slights he receives, and takes his revenge once night falls.

On the Isle of Man, cats that are shut out for the night are said to be on particularly good terms with the fae folk or faeries, sometimes known on the island as Themselves. It was said that the fae would let a cat back inside the house in return, as is customary where the fairy folk are concerned, for an offering, in this case, some of the milk left for the cat.

The Manx cat is also said to be particularly clever – more so than even the average cat. This is because the energy that usually goes into controlling and managing the tail is able to be used by the brain instead!

The Manx cat had various links with fame and celebrity, something that further enhanced their popular status. A visitor to artist J M W Turner in 1810 recorded that the painter had seven cats; they were all tailless, and, according to Turner himself, they came from the Isle of Man.

The folklore of the Manx cat has been delightfully preserved and re-imagined in recent years. In 2012, pupils in Years 5 and 6 at schools on the Isle of Man took part in a competition to write their own origin stories for the Manx cat, in no more than 500 words. The idea behind this was to celebrate the cat's iconic feature, and the heritage and culture of the island in general.

That cats with no tails existed reaching back well into antiquity is evidenced by paintings from ancient Malaysia and China. Other breeds with either truncated or 'missing' tails include the Japanese and American bobtail, the Cymric, Pixie Bob and Highlander.

The island of Reersø, Denmark, is also known for having a population of tailless cats, and although there is no evidence to support this, they are said to be linked to those on the Isle of Man. Stories vary, but it is believed that the cats arrived there between 120 and 200 years ago. One story is that a farmer from Reersø purchased a Manx cat from a sailor; it happened to be pregnant, and her kittens spawned the island's tailless cat population. Another idea involves a shipwreck: according to this tale, a vessel from the Isle of Man was wrecked off the coast of Reersø and the cats on board swam ashore.

The Mystery of the Cabbit

One of the strangest ideas about how the Manx cat came to be is that of the legendary creature known as a Cabbit. According to this theory, Manx cats are actually the product of the unlikely mating of a jack rabbit and a female cat, with the appearance of the Manx cat – hind legs longer than the front, distinctive hopping or lolloping gait and stumpy tail – lending credence to this idea.

The idea was first popularized by antiquarian, writer and poet Joseph Train in his *An Historical and Statistical Account of the Isle of Man* (1845). Here Train stated that: 'My observations on the structure and habits of the specimen in my possession, leave little doubt on my mind of its being a … cross between the female cat and the buck rabbit.'

It is uncertain when the term 'Cabbit' first came into use, but it was potentially when a specimen identified as a Cabbit and named as such, was discovered in New Mexico in 1977. According to the account of Joseph Chapman who discovered the creature, 'It just hopped up in the yard', at the general store he owned near Cuba, New Mexico. Initially thinking it was half-cat, half-rabbit, Chapman took the animal in and gave it a home. According to his account, it had several rabbit-like characteristics, including eating lettuce and cabbage, hopping, and also excreting rabbit-shaped pellets. Chapman, readily admitting that he wanted to make money from his unusual discovery, presented the 'Cabbit' at the Los Angeles Treasure Show, which sparked a great deal of attention on television and in the national press.

According to various experts, however, the creature was not what Chapman claimed it to be, although they were uncertain how to classify it. It was later established that the 'Cabbit' was in fact a domestic cat with a pelvic deformity.

It is believed that the misidentification of the Manx cat accounts for many supposed Cabbit sightings, but this doesn't stop the idea still being a fascination to many, with Cabbits appearing across popular culture, and being particularly popular in anime. The Cabbit is now accepted as purely fictional, and can be seen in the same vein as more famous folkloric animal hybrids, such as the Jackalope.

The Japanese Bobtail

Another cat with a truncated tail is the Japanese Bobtail. With a tail similar to that of a rabbit, the breed was officially registered in the 1960s, but its existence dates back several hundred years.

Intelligent, friendly and communicative, Japanese Bobtails are considered to be very lucky cats, bringing happiness and prosperity to those who own them, with the tri-coloured variety said to be the luckiest of all.

The Old Woman and the Cat

A story from Armenia about how at least one cat lost its tail:

Long ago, an old woman lived alone with her goat. Every day she diligently milked the goat, storing the milk in her cupboard. She was thwarted, however, by a cat that lay in wait each day, sneaking into the cupboard and drinking what she had stored there.

One day, the woman got lucky: she managed to catch the cat, and cut off its tail in punishment for the theft.

'Give me my tail!' the cat cried.

The woman refused, telling the cat she would do so only when the cat brought her milk back.

Determined to be reunited with her tail, the cat visited the goat.

'Please, give me some milk, kind goat! I need it to give to the old woman so she will give me back my tail.'

The goat considered this for a moment. 'If you bring me some boughs from the tree over there, then I will gladly give you milk.'

So the cat journeyed on to where the tree stood, asking politely for some boughs for the goat. 'Please, dear tree, give me some of your boughs! I can then give them to the goat in return for some milk for the old woman, and then I can get my tail back!'

'Bring me some water,' the tree told the cat. 'And then I will give you some boughs.'

And so the cat set off again, this time to the water carrier. 'Oh, kind water carrier! Please give me some water! I will then take it to the tree, who will give some boughs, which I will give to the goat to get some milk, which I will give to the old woman, who will then give me back my tail.'

The water carrier agreed, but only if the cat would bring him some shoes first.

So the cat set off to the shoemaker. 'Good shoemaker! Please, give me a pair of shoes!' And she explained how she would then give them to the water carrier, who would then give him water, and so on, right down to the moment he would, finally, be reunited with her tail.

'Bring me an egg, and I will give you the shoes,' came the shoemaker's reply.

Not to be outdone when so close to achieving his goal, the cat went to see the hen. 'Please, dear hen, give me an egg so that I can give it to the shoemaker, in return for shoes for the water carrier, who will give me water for the tree, who will in return give me some boughs for the goat, who will give me milk for the old woman, so that she might finally give me back my tail.'

Of course, the hen also had a request, telling the cat that she would gladly provide an egg if the cat would bring her some barley.

The cat went straight to the threshing floor. 'Threshing floor, dear, kind threshing floor, give me some barley.'

Finally, the cat was not met with a further request!

'Go ahead,' the threshing floor told the now exhausted cat. 'Gather some barley that my master has left for the birds to eat.'

The cat gathered enough barley and took it to the hen, who then, as agreed, laid an egg. The cat took the egg to the shoemaker and received the shoes, which she took to the water carrier, in return for the water. The water the cat took to the tree, who gave up the requested boughs, and the cat took them to the goat. The goat parted with some milk, which the cat took to the old woman.

'Here is your tail!' the old woman told the cat. 'Now let this be a lesson, and don't go stealing my milk again!'

Overjoyed, the cat was reunited with her tail. But joy soon turned to sorrow, as when the cat tried to attach the tail in its rightful place, it refused to stay. The poor cat tried everything to stick that tail on – resin, tar, glue, anything that might stick – but all in vain.

And that cat has been without a tail ever since – in memory of, and as a sign of, that act of thievery.

A Kink in the Tail

Another variation sometimes seen is the presence of a curve or bend in a cat's tail, a trait particularly common in certain parts of Asia.

One tale often linked to the kinked tail of Siamese cats is that of the bathing princess. One day a princess wished to bathe in a nearby stream but had nowhere to hang her rings. The cat that was with her held out her tail so the princess could slip them over it - alas, the rings would not stay put and kept slipping off. To solve the dilemma, the faithful feline bent her tail so that they would no longer fall off, and so the Siamese had a kinked tail from that day on.

According to one Buddhist legend, nothing on earth could be perfect. The cat however, was dangerously close to perfection, and in order to rectify this issue it was given a kink in the tail.

A similar story focuses on the idea that only perfect things are allowed into heaven. Due to their perfect nature, cats were in danger of causing overcrowding, and so they were either given a bend in their tail to reduce the numbers, or, in another variant, their tails removed altogether so that more of them could fit.

Cats in Folk and Fairy Tales

Reflecting their popularity and prominence in our lives, cats are found throughout folk and fairy tales across the globe in a number of roles and guises. In some stories, cats play a leading role, while in others they might play a smaller, yet still significant part, aiding the protagonist and thus advancing the plot in some vital way.

While each story is unique in and of itself, there are certain common themes and similarities, which can be traced throughout many such tales across different countries and cultures.

The Many Tales of Cats

One common theme in cat-related tales involves a cat or cats that are not actually animals at all, but are bewitched or enchanted humans. Such an example is found in 'Kisa the Cat', a tale from Iceland where the kitten 'Kisa' is revealed to be none other than an enchanted princess, bewitched by a wicked fairy. Similarly, in the French story 'The White Cat', by Madame D'Aulnoy (1698), the white cat is also an enchanted princess; far from being shy and retiring, she shows great spirit, both in ruling her subjects in their feline forms, and in aiding the prince in ultimately fulfilling the tasks necessary to undo the enchantment upon her.

The 'person transformed or bewitched into the form of a cat' theme is also present in some of the many tellings of the well-known fairy tale 'Puss in Boots', of which there are variants in many parts of the world, including Europe, Africa, India and the West Indies. In some versions, the cat is a person who has been enchanted; they are usually freed from the spell by the 'cat' being beheaded and their true identity finally revealed.

A less common role played by a cat is seen in the titular character from the Scottish tale, 'The Black Cat'. In this story, Tom, a lazy farmer's son, enlists in the army in order to avoid, or so he thinks, having to work for a living. He finds himself in more trouble than he bargained for, however, when he is sent overseas and, after suffering at the hands of the abusive local governor, Tom deserts his post and runs away. With desertion punishable by death, he is lucky enough to find help from a kind old woman – possibly a fairy or similar in disguise – who advises him to present his case before the king. Tom does so, and the king sets him a task: he must visit the neighbouring castle and spend the night there. A simple task – but too simple of course!

Before he sets off, the old woman again provides assistance, and advises Tom that when he reaches the castle, he should speak to the black cat that will appear, and ask it for help. Tom does so, and the cat tells him that when it gets dark, three men will come into the room, but that he shouldn't do anything they ask of him. Instead, Tom should wait until someone of greater importance enters – and the cat will let him know who the right person is by touching him.

Sure enough, when night falls three men enter Tom's room, telling him to stand up so that they can sit down. Heeding the cat's advice, Tom stays where he is. Another man then enters and tells Tom to follow him – the cat touches him, so Tom does as the man says. It is lucky that he does, for it turns out that this man is none other than the king of the castle, murdered by the first three men at the behest of his evil steward. The steward, no less, who is the very same governor that Tom had taken issue with previously.

The ghost king tells Tom that he should go and tell his son, who now reigns in his place, everything that he knows. When his death is avenged, the castle will be free of its ghostly inhabitants. Tom does so, and the evil governor gets his comeuppance. Tom becomes governor in his place, and, reunited with his elderly father and now a wealthy man, the story ends happily.

Cats often alter the path of a story for the protagonist, in particular, if the protagonist proves to be worthy of the cat's aid. 'The Two Caskets', a story of Scandinavian origin, is a typical tale of a woman with two daughters – one her own, the other a step-daughter. As is common in tales of this sort, the step-daughter is kind and pretty, but is treated badly by her step-mother, while the daughter, mean-spirited and lazy, is spoiled and indulged.

The mother sets a contest between the two girls: they are handed flax to spin and whoever's thread breaks first is to be pushed down the well. Of course, the odds are stacked heavily against the step-daughter, and she is given poor-quality flax to spin; when her thread breaks, she is duly pushed into the well. When the girl reaches the bottom she is kind to everything and everyone she comes across – from the fence she has to climb over, to the oven that gives her food, to the cow that shares some milk, and when she meets an old woman, she is taken into her service. The girl works hard and does well, and during the course of her daily chores, she gives a 'great company' of cats a daily serving of milk from the cows she tends. In return, these cats help her to complete successfully a series of increasingly difficult tasks set for her by the old woman, who is greatly impressed with her work and clever nature. When it is time for her to finally return home, the old woman allows the girl to choose from a number of caskets to take with her; at the advice of the cats who have grown so fond of her, she chooses one that is revealed to be filled with jewels and great riches.

When the jealous mother sends her own daughter down the well to try and achieve the same result, predictably things don't go to plan. The girl is rude and unpleasant and, as no one likes her, the cats don't provide the same help that they gave her sister. Rather than treasure, her casket contains fire, and when she opens it the house burns down with her and her mother inside, while the good sister is safe with her treasure in the chicken coop.

In the story 'Colony of Cats', a tale believed to have origins on the Italian island of Sicily, the cats involved also further the protagonist's story. There is no indication in this story that the cats are bewitched humans, but they are clearly magical nonetheless. They have the ability to converse with humans as well as holding in their possession two magical jars, and they are also, as in the previous tale, discerning enough to identify and appreciate the true nature of a person.

A great number of cats lived together in a castle. These cats had the power of human speech, and, due to this, were able to employ human servants from the town to keep their abode clean and tidy and to provide them with meals. The cats were exacting masters, however, and due to their high standards, were unable to keep their servants for long, frequently quarrelling with them and then letting them go. One day, young Lizinia – the typical pretty, kind and clever heroine of such a tale – has had enough of the poor treatment meted out to her by her mother and less fair-tempered sister, and leaves home to seek employment at the castle.

Lizinia soon endears herself to her feline employers, and when, after several months of faithful service she decides to return home, the head of the cats, Father Gatto (literally, 'Father Cat') takes her into the cellar and presents her with a choice. There are two earthenware jars there: one containing oil, the other a golden liquid. She can be dipped into one of them – but which will she choose? Lizinia humbly chooses the oil, but Father Gatto tells her that she deserves the gold and proceeds to dip her in that one instead. He then tells her that her wages will be in her pocket when she returns home, and with the instruction to look towards the cock when it crows, but to turn her back on the ass if it brays, he bids her farewell. Lizinia, of course, follows this advice to the letter, earning a silver star on her forehead and golden coins in her pocket every day, much to the annoyance of her family.

As with the previous tale, at the urging of the jealous mother the other sister tries her luck, with the inevitable negative results. Thanks largely to the ever-faithful cats foiling a plot to keep Lizinia from marrying the prince who has fallen in love with her, the protagonist once more lives happily ever after.

In some tales, the cat is a human with the ability to shapeshift, changing their form at will. In such stories, this is usually an individual of a questionable nature, often a witch or bad-natured fairy, seeking to do ill. In some stories involving the iconic witch figure of Slavic folklore, Baba Yaga, she is portrayed as having a cat or cat companions, again reinforcing the historical link between cats and witches.

Not all cats in fairy and folk tales are magical in some way. In 'Two Kind Cats', a tale from Italy, when a merchant visits a land devastated by mice, he sets his two treasured cats free to take care of the problem, and the king expresses his gratitude with a variety of gifts. When the man returns home with these riches, another merchant is overcome with envy and goes there himself, taking fine silks and fabrics. The king and his advisors cannot rival these and have nothing suitable to trade, until one of them comes up with a solution – two of the original cats' kittens – as they were the greatest gift that they had ever received on the island. The merchant returns home, suitably humbled and having learned a valuable lesson: that to receive good things and happiness, it is necessary to first give them to others.

A cat is often a companion to the main protagonist in a story, again seen in 'Puss in Boots' and the many variants of this tale. This is also the case in 'The Clever Cat'. A prince owns a magical stone that grants his wishes; when the stone falls into the hands of an evil ogre, the prince, along with his faithful falcon, greyhound and cat, sets off on a mission to retrieve it. The falcon and cat are sent out to locate the ogre; when they pass over a city of rats, it is the cat who takes charge, sitting outside the gates and engaging with the rats, ultimately securing the stone when the rats burrow under the walls of the castle and steal it from the ogre.

In a common motif of an item gained and then lost again, on the way home, the cat, holding the stone in his mouth, is being carried by the falcon. A disagreement breaks out when they stop to rest for the night, as the falcon wants a turn to watch the stone, saying that, so far, the cat has done everything. When the cat opens her mouth to argue back, she drops the stone, and it bounces out of reach, landing in the river, in the ear of a large fish, who then swims away.

Again, the cat shows her resourcefulness, digging up the bank and throwing the dirt into the stream. Alerted by the disturbance, a fish asks her to stop choking up the water but the cat refuses; explaining that she will only stop digging if the fish finds the stone for her. Luckily for all, the fish happens to know of a great tuna that travels far and wide and has such great wisdom that he is sure to know the location of the stone. Upon finding him, however, it transpires that the stone had actually fallen into the ear of this very same tuna. The cat and the stone are thus reunited, the stone is returned to the prince and all is well.

Through living alongside them for so many years, humankind has come to observe and predict certain characteristics where the cat is concerned, and these are often reflected in the fairy and folk tales that feature them.

In many tales, cats are portrayed as clever and intelligent, with the ability to solve problems and think outside the box. Sometimes this means that the cat is portrayed as particularly sly or cunning, getting the better of an animal that is, in contrast, depicted as less intelligent or more gullible. Another trait that is often attributed to cats in general is that of being lazy, due to their fondness for sleeping for much of the day, lounging in the sun or in front of the fire.

The relationship between cats and other animals – most commonly their habitual foes, dogs and mice – also features frequently in cat-related tales. In many such stories, dog and cat start out as friends, until something occurs that disrupts this accord and turns them into eternal enemies.

In 'Why Dogs Dislike Cats and Cats Dislike Mice', Dog once served Lion, the King of the Animals, most faithfully for years. Wanting to reward this dedicated service, Lion proclaims Dog a noble, giving him a parchment scroll to confirm this great honour. Very proud, Dog races to tell his good friend Cat, who he then tasks with looking after the parchment. Cat agrees, and stores it safely away in a great oak tree. Cat checks on it regularly to start with, but as time goes by, does so less and less, until she forgets to check on it all together. Unbeknown to them, one day a small mouse discovers the hiding place, and, over many visits, enjoys a good nibble of the precious document, until it is quite ruined.

When Dog inevitably comes to Cat to ask for the document back, so he can take it to a tournament, the terrible truth is discovered. Cat is angry with the mouse and declares everlasting enmity towards it. Dog does likewise with Cat, and it has been thus ever since.

In other stories, the discord between cat and dog is caused by the preferential treatment of humans towards one or the other: for instance, in one story from China, the master feeds cats fresh fish, while only giving bones to the dogs, which sets them at odds with one another. This is also seen in a story from Korea where a cat and dog team up to retrieve a stolen iron measure that was the source of their master's prosperity. They are successful, but manage to lose the item again on the way home. After various incidents, the pair manage to retrieve it, but when they return home, because the cat was the one holding it, she is rewarded and allowed to sleep on the bed, whereas the dog is left to sleep in the yard. Due to this injustice, the dog has barked at the cat to this day.

Why Cats Always Wash After Eating

Cats are well known for being fastidious when it comes to cleanliness, and it's a common sight to see a cat giving itself a good wash, particularly after a meal. But have you ever wondered exactly why a cat cleans itself after eating? A folk tale from Belgium gives us one explanation for this familiar habit.

Many, many years ago, a cat, as cats do, was hunting a sparrow, and, after much determination, managed to catch his prey. He toyed with it a while, drawing out the anticipation, imagining how good it would taste when he finally swallowed it down.

All of a sudden, the sparrow spoke.

Did he know, the sparrow asked, that the fine cat living in the Emperor's household would never dream of eating before washing itself first? Furthermore, the Emperor himself and all of his family likewise washed themselves before starting to eat their food. It was customary, and no one in polite society with any manners would dream of eating before doing so.

The cat, rather taken aback, considered the matter. He had never imagined that such a thing might make a difference, but, if it was good enough for the Emperor's cat, then it was good enough for him, and he would follow the example set by his betters.

With that resolution firmly in mind, the cat lifted his paw to wash his face in preparation for eating the tasty morsel before him. But oh, alas for the cat! For the very moment he lifted that paw, the sparrow seized the chance it had been waiting for and flew away to safety. There it sat, perched on a branch far out of reach, silently watching its former captor.

How the cat rued the moment he had listened to that sparrow! Vowing never to be deceived in such a way again, from then on, this cat – and all cats – make sure to wash after eating.

Why Dog Chases Cat

Of all the relationships between animals, the well-known animosity between cat and dog is among the most established. This tale of African American origin offers one explanation for why these two are mortal enemies:

Dog and Cat were once next door neighbours. Contrary to how it often is today, the pair were good friends, the very best in fact. For they had a favourite activity that they shared in common: eating. And their favourite thing to eat was ham. So fond of ham were they that whenever there was money to spare, they each bought a slice of ham.

One day, Dog came to Cat and said, 'We've got some extra money I see, but there isn't enough to buy a whole ham each. If, however, we put our money together, then we could buy a large ham to share between us!'

Cat was very keen on this idea, and heartily agreed, so the pair set off into town without further ado. There, they bought the largest, juiciest ham they could find. It was so heavy that neither of them could carry it for long, and they had to share the delicious burden, taking it in turns to carry it on the walk home.

In anticipation of the fine meal they were to share, as he carried the joint, Dog sang, 'Our ham, our ham, our ham.'

Then Cat took a turn. The delicious scent of the ham was tempting and enticing, and she found herself thinking, 'I would really like to have this entire ham as my own.' With that thought in her mind, Cat sang, 'My ham, my ham, my ham.'

Now, this made Dog somewhat suspicious. He kept quiet, however, and again, when it was his turn to carry the ham, sang 'Our ham, our ham, our ham.'

So they carried on their way, and, as they drew closer to home, Cat once again carried the ham, and, again, sang, 'My ham, my ham, my ham.' Then, before Dog could do anything about it, she leapt up into the nearest tree, and began to devour the ham.

Dog, unable to climb the tree, was helpless to do anything about it. He had to sit there, beneath the tree, looking on as Cat ate all the ham. It made him so angry, and with each passing moment he grew angrier and angrier, barking louder and louder in his rage.

The remorseless Cat just kept on going, and when the ham was all gone, smacked her lips together in appreciation and rubbed her stomach.

Enraged, Dog yelled, 'Cat! You'd better watch out! Because when you get hungry again and have to come down from that tree, I'm going to eat you!'

Of course, Cat did grow hungry again, and did have to come down from the tree. Dog chased after her, and from that day on, Dog has chased Cat whenever he sees her, all over that stolen joint of ham.

Bayun the Cat

One of the most renowned cats in Russian and Slavic folklore today is Bayun the Cat or Cat Bayun.

According to generally held ideas, Bayun is a masterful storyteller and singer. He is said to sit on a high pole, most often made of iron, or sometimes gold, and he lives in the 'thirtieth kingdom', or deep in a forest that is devoid of most signs of life.

In some stories, Bayun is a giant, man-eating cat, both charming and deadly in equal measure. His voice is said to be one of his most notable attributes: soothing and cajoling, he uses it to read an endless supply of fairy tales and songs, and is said to be so loud that it carries from three miles away when he is telling his stories.

Capturing or securing Bayun is a quest in many a tale, but it is no easy feat to accomplish. In one story, the protagonist resorts to iron gloves and an iron cap in order to tackle the notorious creature, both to protect himself against being scratched by the animal's sharp claws, or being put to sleep by his magical voice – it is said that Bayun's voice has a strongly soporific quality and can put people to sleep from a great distance before they have even set eyes on him.

The name Bayun is believed to come from the Russian verb *bayut* – meaning 'to tell' or 'to speak'. Interestingly, given that

Bayun's voice is often said to have soporific qualities, it may also stem from the verb *bayukat* – which means 'to put to sleep'.

The exact origins of the character Bayun are unknown. He is often linked to the older idea of 'the learned cat' within Russian literature. For example, although not explicitly named as Bayun, a cat is mentioned in the prologue to Alexander Pushkin's 19th-century epic poem, *Ruslan and Ludmila*, of whom it is said:

There's a green oak by the bay,
And a learned cat walks round and round;
It walks to the right — it sings a song, It walks to the left – it tells a tale …

This cat is generally thought to be either Bayun himself, or a forerunner to the popular character.

The first properly traceable existence of Bayun as a character comes from the 19th-century collections of Alexander Afanasyev published between 1855 and 1867, where he is mentioned in various tales. Bayun is noticeably absent from earlier volumes of fairy tales. The only mention before Afanasyev appears to be in *Tales of the Russian People*, by I P Sakharov (1848).

It has been suggested that Bayun did not actually come to prominence until the Soviet era, beginning in 1922. It was then that Bayun was included in the 'national bestiary' of popular folkloric characters such as Baba Yaga.

Over time, Bayun has reached an audience far beyond his original roots, and today can be found in various popular media, including the video game *The Tales of Bayun*, where he imparts knowledge in return for a price. He has also influenced popular music, including a folk-metal band called Kot-Bayu with a song about the cat, and an artist known as Bayun the Cat.

Kisa the Cat

Collected in *Die neuisländischen Volksmärchen* (1902) by Adeline Rittershaus and later adapted and published by Andrew Lang in *The Brown Fairy Book*, 1904.

There was once a queen, and that queen owned a cat. The cat was beautiful to behold, with smoke-coloured fur and eyes as blue as china. The queen and the cat were the firmest of friends, the cat her constant companion, following the queen as she went here and there. The queen was so fond of her feline companion, that she even allowed her to sit beside her when she went out in her gleaming glass coach.

Despite their friendship, however, the queen was sad. One day, when they were out for their customary drive, she revealed this to the cat, telling her faithful pet that she was sure the cat was much happier than she, for the cat had a little kitten in her own likeness, while the queen had no one to call her own save for the cat.

'Don't cry,' said the cat, and, much moved, placed a comforting paw against her mistress's arm. For, the cat went on, crying would do no good. Instead, she, the cat, would see what she could do about the situation.

The cat kept her promise, and, once they returned home, she set off to solve this problem for her mistress. The little cat made her way towards the forest, where a fairy lived, and consulted with her at length. Whatever was said, it had the desired result, as not long after this, the queen gave birth to a baby girl. The baby was very precious indeed, seeming for all the world as if she were made of the finest snow and sunbeams imaginable. How happy the queen was!

It was not long before the baby, growing more aware of her surroundings each day, became aware of the cat's own kitten, and the two became firm friends, in the same way that the cat and the queen were to each other. The child was so enamoured of the kitten that she would roam around when she should be in bed, refusing to sleep unless the kitten was curled up tightly beside her.

Now, kittens grow much more quickly than human babies, and although the baby was still small, the kitten was now more cat than kitten. One evening, the nurse came to look for the kitten to put in with the baby to sleep, but alas! The kitten-cat was nowhere to be found. An anxious search ensued, with servants hunting high and low for the treasured companion. First they checked all of the obvious places, and then they checked the less obvious, searching everywhere from the drawers in the kitchen to the snuggest corner that the cat might have squeezed into. All to no avail. It was as if the kitten had vanished. It had, they all concluded, run away, and whether it would choose to return was anybody's guess.

Days turned into months and months into years, and the young princess grew into a fine young child. One day when she was playing with her ball in the palace gardens, she accidentally threw it further than usual. The ball flew out of sight, and dropped into some rose bushes; with a child's impulsiveness the princess ran to find it, hunting in the long grass on her knees. The girl felt around, trying to find the ball, when all of a sudden she heard a voice, calling her name.

'Ingibjorg! Ingibjorg!'

The girl listened, as the voice continued, 'Have you forgotten me? I am Kisa, your sister!'

The girl was very confused, for, as far as she was aware, she had no sister. She had, of course, been far too young to remember the small kitten who had been her constant companion during her first months of life, and as no one had thought to tell her of what had happened, she was none the wiser.

'But do you not remember?' the cat asked indignantly, shaking its head at the short memories of girls. It used to sleep beside her in her cot, it told her, and even now, it could find its way up to that very room if allowed inside.

'Why then did you leave?' the girl wanted to know. Kisa started to answer, but at that moment the girl's attendants appeared, breathless from hurrying to find their wayward charge. They were horrified to find the girl talking to a strange cat, and Kisa darted away, through the bushes and back towards the forest from where she had come.

The following morning dawned very hot. The princess, still thinking of Kisa, decided that the forest was where she would play that day, under the shade of the large trees that would shelter her from the sun. She was indulged, as usual, by her ladies-in-waiting, who allowed her to do as she pleased, unless it was something that would lead to harm. The attendants settled themselves beside a small stream, tinkling gently by, and, in the cool, shady forest, they were soon fast asleep. Knowing full well that she could now do whatever she wanted, the princess wandered further and further, exploring where she had not been before. Perhaps, she thought, she might come across fairies dancing in a ring, or elves, watching her as she went, or some other pleasant and magical sight. But it was not to be; far from it, in fact, for instead she encountered a large, ill-tempered giant as he lumbered from his cave, and, spying the princess, demanded that she follow him. Terrified and regretting that she had wandered so far away, the princess did not dare to disobey such a large, terrible creature, and reluctantly followed behind him.

The giant continued for such a distance that the young Ingibjorg felt very, very, weary indeed. She was so worn out that, despite her fear of the giant, she started to cry.

The giant, heartless and irritated, turned to face her. 'I don't like girls who make such horrible noise,' he told her with a growl. Worse was to come though, as, drawing an axe from his belt, he added, 'If you want to cry, then I will give you something to cry about!' And with that, he cut off both of her feet. Without a word, he picked up those poor little feet, put them in his pocket, and walked off, leaving the princess crying and bleeding in the grass where she had fallen.

Poor Ingibjorg! It felt like a lifetime ago since she had left home that morning, and she had no idea how far she had come. No one would know where to look for her; she thought she might end up lying there, alone and in agony, until she died.

After a time – and it cannot have been too great a time, as the sun was still high in the sky – the sound of wheels penetrated through the poor princess's misery. Using all of her strength, her throat parched and hoarse, she cried out, hoping that whoever it was might hear her.

'I am coming!' the answer came immediately, and a moment later, a cart appeared, driving through the trees, driven by none other than Kisa. As soon as she saw her friend, the cat leapt down from the cart. With tender paws, Kisa lifted the girl, laying her gently on a bed of hay in the cart, before driving away into the forest to where she had a hut of her own.

Though nowhere near as luxurious as the palace that was her home, to Ingibjorg, the pile of cushions Kisa laid her upon were the most heavenly she had ever beheld. Close to fainting, she drank down the milk she was offered, before settling as comfortably as she could onto the makeshift bed. Meanwhile, Kisa worked with great industry; gathering some dried herbs from her cupboards, she soaked them in warm water before gently tying them to the girl's pitifully bleeding legs. To her amazement, the pain vanished immediately, and Ingibjorg smiled in gratitude and relief.

Kisa left her to sleep, intent upon her mission. Wasting no time, she leapt up into her cart, grabbing the reins, and heading off into the forest, making directly for the giant's cave. When she arrived, the cat hid her cart a little distance off behind some trees, making sure it couldn't be seen. With all the stealth that a cat knows, Kisa crept towards the door and crouched down; as the door was ajar, she was able to listen to the giant and his wife talking over supper.

'I shall go back and kill the girl the moment I have time,' the giant declared. For it would not do at all for anyone in the forest to know that a child of all things had managed to defy him. What would that do to his reputation! The wife agreed wholeheartedly, and the pair continued to discuss the princess, calling her all manner of horrible names and lamenting her unfortunate behaviour. So intent on their talk were they that they paid no heed to Kisa as she crept carefully and quietly, unseen, into the cottage to where a bag of salt lay. Swiftly, the cat upended the bag into the large cooking pot by the fire, until not one grain remained, before quickly slinking out again.

Presently, the giant and his wife helped themselves to more soup, eating greedily. It might have been wiser to have eaten more slowly, as within moments the giant was crying out that he was very, very, thirsty.

'As am I!' his wife agreed, for the salt had done its job and left them parched and dry.

'I must have water right now, otherwise I will die!' the giant declared dramatically, before, pushing back his chair, dashing from the cave, with his wife close behind.

The watchful Kisa seized her moment and set to work. She hunted everywhere, in every crevice and cranny, until, finally, she spotted some grass lying in the corner. Lifting it, she discovered what she was looking for: Ingibjorg's severed feet lay safe and sound beneath it. Kisa quickly gathered them up, setting them in her cart, and drove off back to her hut and the waiting girl.

The princess was very pleased to see Kisa, as although exhausted, she had been too frightened to sleep for long, worrying with every crack and creak outside that the giant was coming for her to finish the job he had started. She was even more overjoyed when Kisa, entering the hut, held up her poor feet, still encased in their pretty silver slippers.

'Do not fear, for in two minutes we shall have these feet back as ever they were!' Kisa told her confidently. The giant's grass was magical, and Kisa skillfully used it to tie Ingibjorg's feet back in place. She wouldn't, Kisa warned, be able to walk properly for a while, as it would take some time for them to heal enough for her to use again. But, if she rested and did as Kisa told her, in a week or so it might be possible to return home again.

The girl resolved to do as she was bidden, and a week or so later, Kisa was as good as her word. The cat gently helped the princess into the cart once more, before driving her old friend homewards, lashing the horse with her tail as they drove for the palace.

How amazed and delighted the king and queen were to see their daughter returning to them! There was no reward, they declared, too great for the one who had returned her to them and saved her from certain death.

Kisa, however, was in no hurry to discuss such matters. After handing the princess over, she bowed elegantly and headed on her way. Poor Ingibjorg was most upset that Kisa had left again, even more so that she had not even said goodbye. She took it so much to heart that she could not eat or drink; she was listless and unhappy and showed no interest in anything, in spite of all the fine dresses and other distractions her parents heaped upon her.

The king and queen grew more and more worried, as day by day the princess showed no sign of improvement, or interest in anything. In time, they became convinced that she would die if some remedy did not present itself, and they thought and thought of something that had not so far been tried to rouse the wasting girl.

Finally the king realized there was one thing they had not tried: marriage. In desperation, he wasted no time summoning every unmarried young man throughout the land that might make a suitable match for his daughter. Ingibjorg was brought to meet them, in the hope there might be one whom she would wish to marry.

There were many fine and interesting young men, princes and lords among them, and Ingibjorg spent a great deal of time deliberating. There was one young man, kind and gentle, whom she liked a great deal, and who returned her affections. As everyone had hoped, with companionship and interest, the girl began to recover her former good spirits, and in time, a fine wedding was held and the two became husband and wife. It suited the king especially, as her choice happened to be the son of a neighbouring king, thus uniting their two lands and families. There was a magnificent feast and much celebrating.

At the end of the wedding, who should appear but Kisa! The princess was overjoyed, and rushed to hug the cat tightly.

'I have come to claim my reward,' Kisa told her. Anything, she was told without hesitation. But, it turned out, the reward Kisa wanted was to sleep that night at the foot of Ingibjorg's bed.

'Is that all?' the princess couldn't believe what she was hearing. Surely Kisa wanted something much more than that? But no, Kisa assured her, that was enough indeed, and she wanted nothing more.

And so Kisa slept the night at the foot of the princess's bed. But come morning, there was no cat to be found there. Instead, to everyone's amazement, there lay a beautiful princess in her place. How could this be?

Kisa – for it was she – explained her whole story. 'Long ago,' the girl explained, 'My mother and I were enchanted by a spiteful fairy. The only way we could hope to free ourselves from the curse was to carry out a kind deed that had never been done before. We tried and tried, but my poor mother died before she was able to break the curse upon herself. Thanks to the evil deed the giant performed upon you, however, I was able to make you whole again, and thus break the curse upon myself and be human again.'

How delighted everyone was to hear this! The princess stayed with Ingibjorg and the prince and the court, and everyone was most happy. Eventually Kisa herself married, and governed her own lands for many, many years to come.

How the Pussy Willow Got Its Name

The pussy willow is a popular symbol of spring and Easter in the United States and across many areas of Europe. In Poland, on Palm Sunday, willow branches are used in place of palms. After the bleak, cold days of winter, the appearance of the grey, furry buds of the pussy willow are one of the first welcome signs that spring is finally on the way.

One spring day, three young kittens were playing together on the banks of a river. They pranced and frolicked, darting back and forth as they cavorted merrily along, without a care in the world. Their mother watched from a distance, gently cautioning them not to stray too close to the water's edge. But alas! Her warning was not heeded, and the three tumbled straight into the water.

The small, helpless creatures were swept away on the current, their frantic mother running alongside, crying out in distress for someone to help her. There was no one around to heed her cries, however, and the sodden bundles mewled most pitifully as they were carried along, close to drowning.

But rescue came from an unexpected quarter. Just as they believed all was lost, the willow trees on the river bank heard the mother cat's desperate pleas. Bending low, they reached their

branches down into the water, calling for the kittens to hold on. With the last of their failing strength, they managed to do so, and were hauled to safety.

There were no words to express the mother cat's gratitude as she was reunited with her precious kittens, licking them dry as they clung to the branches of the trees that had saved their lives.

Every year from that day forth, to commemorate this heroic rescue, the willow grows tiny soft, grey buds in memory of the kittens that were saved.

The tale above, said to have originated in Poland, is just one explanation for how the pussy willow came to be so named. There are other variations of this origin story, and not all have such a happy ending. In one from parts of Scandinavia, the kittens find themselves trapped outside in the harsh winter snow, and try to find shelter by climbing the willow. They perish, but their tails sprout into catkins on the branches of the trees every year from that time on.

This connection between cats and the willow tree is an old one: the word 'catkin' comes from the old Dutch word for kitten, *katteken*.

Although we tend to refer to the pussy willow as if it is a single species, there are in fact several trees that are known by this name when they are in bud: the goat willow (Europe and western and central Asia), grey willow (Europe and western Asia) and American pussy willow (North America) are all referred to as pussy willow due to their buds or catkins covered in fine grey fur.

The King of the Cats

There are many variations of this tale found across England, Scotland and Ireland, the earliest dating from the 18th century. The name of the cats involved and the circumstances may differ, but the end result is generally the same as in the version that follows.

One cold, winter's night, a sexton's wife sat dozing by the fire, with the family cat, Old Tom, snoozing on the rug before her. They were waiting for the master of the house to return home, but something had clearly delayed him, for they waited and waited, and still he did not appear.

Just as the woman was starting to worry, the door burst open and in ran her husband.

'Who is Tommy Tildrum?' he demanded.

Her tiredness forgotten, the wife leapt to her feet. 'What has happened? And why do you ask such a question?'

'I was busy digging the grave for tomorrow's funeral, but due to the late hour, I must have fallen asleep. Suddenly, a loud "Miaow" woke me – and you'll never guess what I saw as I looked up over the edge of that grave!'

'What?' demanded his wife, now greatly alarmed.

'Nine black cats!' the man declared wildly. 'Nine black cats were there, each with a white spot on their chest, and you'll never guess

what they were carrying!'

'What were they carrying?' the woman demanded, growing more and more worried by the second.

'A small coffin! It was the smallest one you ever saw, covered with black velvet and on top of that a little gold crown!'

'As they came closer, I could see their eyes were shining green – eight of them carrying the coffin, the ninth walking in front. They spotted me and just stopped and stared at me – the one at the front came up to me and told me to tell Tom Tildrum that Tom Toidrum is dead. But how am I supposed to know who Tom Tildrum is?'

Now the cat had been watching and listening to this exchange the whole time, an alert and interested expression on his face. But when the wife caught sight of him she let out a shriek. For Tom the cat was no longer the size he had been before. Tom was growing and growing, and finally let out a cry of his own.

'What, Old Tom is dead? Then that means I am now King of the Cats!' And with that, before anyone could stop him, he vanished up the chimney, and they never saw him again.

Grinning Like a Cheshire Cat

The image of the Cheshire Cat, with its wide, trademark smile and habit of slowly vanishing and reappearing seemingly at will, is one of the most recognizable and popular characters from Lewis Carroll's much-loved *Alice's Adventures in Wonderland* (1865).

Although the idea of the Cheshire Cat and its famous smile is often attributed to Carroll, the phrase 'grinning like a Cheshire Cat' was actually well known long before the book's publication, and the character was, in fact, a play on an existing figure of speech.

What might have inspired Carroll has been hotly debated, as have the origins of the phrase itself.

The phrase 'to grin like a Cheshire Cat' dates to at least the late 18th century: the earliest recorded mention is from around 1770, but it was most likely an established phrase well before this. An entry for 'Cheshire Cat' in Francis Grose's *A Classical Dictionary of the Vulgar Tongue* (1788) reads: '"He grins like a Cheshire cat", said of anyone who shows his teeth and gums in laughing.'

Other sources for the term that pre-date Carroll include a letter written in 1806 by English essayist and poet Charles

Lamb to his close friend Thomas Manning, where Lamb remarks, 'I made a pun the other day, and palmed it upon Holcroft, who grinned like a Cheshire cat. (Why do cats grin in Cheshire? – Because it was once a county palatine, and the cats cannot help laughing whenever they think of it, though I see no great joke in it.)'

This refers to the fact that in the medieval period, Chester – along with Durham and Lancaster – had the rare privilege of not being subject to the king's writ: an official order backed by the king's power. In such areas, royal privileges and rights of jurisdiction were held instead by the lord or earl of the county, meaning that, in theory at least, anyone who had committed a crime elsewhere and managed to find themselves across the border would be safe from prosecution.

The saying has also been linked to an older, more gruesome, turn of phrase. The 'Cheshire grin' or 'Cheshire smile' was used to refer to the cutting of someone's throat from ear to ear. In a similar vein, it has been suggested that the phrase originated in the sight of the severed heads of executed criminals displayed on poles above the gates of Chester Castle.

There is an issue with the majority of these potential origins, however; namely that they don't involve something that is specific to Cheshire itself, and therefore they do not adequately explain why cats from Cheshire specifically are said to be grinning.

One theory that at least attempts to address this dilemma is the idea that Cheshire cheeses, for which the county is renowned, used to be sold in the shape of a cat. Although this claim was made in the mid-19th century, unfortunately this can't be confirmed by any earlier sources, and it is therefore likely that said cheese advertising came after the saying was already established, capitalizing on a phrase that was already well known.

Another explanation that could hold more weight is also linked to the dairy produce of the area. Cheshire has been renowned for its cheese and milk since at least the 12th century, and if any cat had been lucky enough to gain access to such high-quality produce, it would have been particularly pleased – and may well have been grinning having managed to lap some of the milk before being chased away.

What inspired Carroll to use both the phrase and a cat to create his character is also hotly debated. The first thing to note is that the phrase does not refer to a specific type of cat; there is no such breed as a 'Cheshire cat', so this couldn't have been the source of Carroll's idea. There is, however, the British Shorthair: with their distinctively rounded heads and big cheeks, British Shorthairs do, at times, appear to have a contented or even smug grin on their faces, and it has been suggested that the British Shorthair may have inspired Carroll.

It has also been suggested that Carroll was influenced by one or more stone carvings of cats that he is said to have connections with. One popular candidate is the stone cat head located in the church of St Nicolas, Cranleigh, Surrey. However, it was not until after the publication of *Alice* that Carroll moved to nearby Guildford, and so this is a less viable candidate than it originally appears. Another oft-cited contender is the smiling sandstone cat on the tower of St Wilfrid's Church, Grappenhall, Cheshire, which happens to be close to Carroll's birthplace, Daresbury in Warrington.

Yet another theory is that the slow disappearance and equally slow return of the cat in the story reflects the phases of the waning and waxing moon.

Conclusion: Celebrating Cats – Past, Present and Future

It seems fitting to end this book with a look at some of the many ways that cats are celebrated and enjoyed today.

It is an inescapable fact that, throughout history, cats have frequently received less than kind treatment. Some of our modern festivals and traditions have developed from such earlier beliefs and practices, and nowadays are used to highlight the importance of treating cats with kindness and respect.

Kattenstoet ('Cat Parade') is a festival held every three years in the city of Ieper (Ypres), Belgium. Running since 1955, it traditionally takes place on the second Sunday in May, and the community and family-oriented parade that makes up the main element of the festival today is said to commemorate a far darker tradition dating from the medieval period, when cats were hurled down into the square from the belfry tower of the Cloth Hall located in the Grote Markt in the centre of the city.

There are different theories and legends associated with the origins of this practice. One popular idea is that cats were brought to the Cloth Hall in order to control the number of rodents. During the colder months, the cloth that was stored there, and thus the cats, would be moved to the higher floors; when the weather warmed up in the spring and the cloth was sold, the cats were no longer needed, and surplus to requirements, were hurled from the tower.

Another theory links the practice to the long-held connection between cats and witches. It has been suggested that cats were thrown from the tower because they were considered evil, in an attempt to rid the city of evil spirits and break the power of witches.

Readers will be relieved to learn that it is believed that the last live cat was thrown from the tower in 1817, and the event held today is a far cry from these less humane origins. Now, an individual dressed as a jester climbs to the top of the belfry tower; then, watched by the eager crowds below, the jester flings down stuffed toy cats, which are caught by lucky onlookers. This is followed by a mock witch burning, with a puppet witch set on fire in front the crowds, a ritual that alludes to the perceived close association between cats and witches. The event is a popular one in the locality, attracting upwards of 2,000 people, and familiar and popular characters sometimes make an appearance: At Kattenstoet 2024, Musti – the famous Belgian comic cat – joined the parade to the delight of many.

Russia has an enduring history and fascination with cats, as reflected by their appearance in many tales and folklore. The Hermitage Museum in St Petersburg has a long historical association with cats, a connection that is said to have been first established in 1745, when Elizabeth of Russia, Empress from 1741 to 1762, introduced cats into the Winter Palace that adjoins The Hermitage, to deal with the increasing rodent population. Today, cats reside in the basement of the building, and can also be seen enjoying the sun in the nearby square or on the river embankment during the warmer months of the year. The Hermitage cats are minor celebrities in their own right, with their own press secretary and three caretakers; thousands of tourists flock to see them each year.

Every year, the Winter Palace organizes a well-deserved celebration for these famed felines known as Day of the Hermitage Cat. Organized for the first time in 1998, it became an annual and international event from 2005. Also known as March Cat Day, family orientated activities and events are held by the museum, including an art competition and children's activities such as scavenger hunts. For those who can't stand to leave these cats behind at the end of their visit, a more permanent arrangement is possible, as all of the 60–80 cats at the Hermitage are available for adoption.

The importance of cats is also reflected in the number of 'cat days' celebrated across the world. International Cat Day is celebrated on 8 August. It was created by the International Fund for Animal Welfare, to raise general awareness of cats and issues regarding cat protection, and first took place in 2002. Since 2020, it has been overseen by the British non-profit organization International Cat Care, which was established in 1958 to improve the health and welfare of domestic cats.

In Russia, National Cat Day is celebrated on 1 March, reflecting the fact that in Russian culture cats are seen as a symbol of spring, and March in general is often referred to as Cat Month. It was established in 2004 by the Moscow Museum of Cats and the editorial board of the magazine *Cat and Dog*, and quickly became established as an unofficial holiday, marked by many across the country.

In Japan, 22 February marks National Cat Day. It has been celebrated on this date since 1978 when it was chosen by the Executive Cat Day Committee due to the fact that 22/2 – *nyan, nyan, nyan* in Japanese – is similar to the sound of a cat: 'meow, meow, meow'. The day is marked in a variety of ways, with local businesses selling cat-themed food and merchandise, and people sharing pictures of themselves with their cats across social media.

In the United States, National Cat Day is 29 October, and Canada celebrates it on 8 August. In both countries, the aim of the day is to raise awareness of and promote the importance of cat adoption.

National Cat Day in Italy, Poland and Brazil is 17 February, and fundraising campaigns are held to raise money for animal shelters. Australia marks the event on 29 October.

Celebrations of all things feline have increased greatly over recent years, further reflecting the prominent place cats hold in our lives. The first New York Cat Film Festival took place in December 2017, and has been an annual event since then. Founded by Tracie Hotchner, author and pet wellness advocate, the festival tours various locations across the country with the dual purpose of celebrating everything that is wonderful about our feline companions while also educating and raising awareness. The festival also helps to raise money for local animal welfare charities.

And so we come to the end of our journey through some of the most fascinating feline-folklore down the ages. From gods to ghosts to folk and fairy tales, one thing is undeniable: in words that are often attributed to the late and great Terry Pratchett, 'In ancient times cats were worshipped as gods; they have not forgotten this.'

Long may it continue.

ACKNOWLEDGEMENTS

As always, when it comes to this part of the book-writing process, it is impossible to name everyone who has helped see me through, and the acknowledgements that follow only scratch the tip of the iceberg when it comes to my appreciation.

First, a massive and heartfelt thank you to everyone who continues to read my books: whether this is your first one, or if you've been with me since the beginning, without you, I wouldn't be able to continue to do the things I love – researching and writing books. Thank you!

Thank you to everyone at Batsford Books for giving me the opportunity to bring this book into the world, and for all of the ongoing support and tireless hard work that goes on behind the scenes – thank you!

Massive thanks as always to the wonderfully knowledgeable and patient Mark Norman for proofreading, the bouncing around of ideas, and general advice and sanity-saving throughout the process, including teaching me how to actually use voice notes.

I am also hugely indebted to Dee Dee Chainey for her steadfast support and encouragement: the best friendships are indeed built on a solid foundation of a shared taste in memes, and may that never change.

Thanks also goes to each of my three children: for their unique and wonderful personalities and the fact that they are still always so very excited to see my books out in the wild.

Thank you also to my wonderful Emma-Loola and her fabulous Mowie – no other cat could take mealtime surveillance as seriously as he does.

And last but not least, a big shout out to our own wonderful cats – Hector and Jayfeather, our lives would not be complete without you and we are honoured that you consider us your adoring hoomans. (Though I stand by the fact that chewing my notes and sitting on my laptop is not the way to 'help' me get work done!)

SELECTED FURTHER READING

It isn't possible to list all of the reference material used for this book; however, here is a selection of sources that may interest readers who would like to know more about some of the themes in this book.

Addy, S O, *Household Tales: Traditional Remains of York, Lincoln, Derby and Nottingham*. David Nutt, London, 1895

Alford, Violet, 'The Cat Saint'. *Folklore*, vol. 52, no. 3, 1941, pp.161–83. JSTOR, http://www.jstor.org/stable/1257493. Accessed 19 April 2025

Attalus.org, *Egyptian Texts* 1.16: The Myth of the Solar Eye. https://www.attalus.org/egypt/solar_eye.html

Briggs, Katherine, *A Dictionary of British Folk-Tales in the English Language*. Four volumes. Routledge & Kegan Paul, London, 1970

Briggs, Katherine, *Nine Lives: The Folklore of Cats*. Dorset Press, New York, 1980

Buchan, Peter and Lawrence, Rachel Louise, *Ancient Scottish Tales, Traditional, Romantic & Legendary Folk and Fairy Tales of the Highlands*. Blackdown Publications, 2019

Bunson, Margaret R, The Encyclopedia of Ancient Egypt, Facts on File Publications, New York, 1991

Champion, Selwyn Gurney, M D, *Racial Proverbs: A Selection of the World's Proverbs Arranged Linguistically*. London, Routledge, 1938

Dassent, G W, *Tales from the Norse*. David Douglas, Edinburgh, 1903

Davisson, Zack, *Kaibyo: Supernatural Cats of Japan*, Chin Music Press Inc., Seattle, 2017

Engels, D, *Classical Cats: The Rise and Fall of the Sacred Cat*. London and New York, Routledge, 1999

Ganguli, Kisari Mohan (trans), *The Mahabharata*, Book 12: Santi Parva, https://sacred-texts.com/hin/m12/m12a137.htm

Goodwins, Sara, *A De-tailed Account of Manx Cats*. Loaghtan Books, Isle of Man, 2013

Goss, Michael, 'Alien Big Cat Sightings in Britain: A Possible

Rumour Legend?' Folklore, 103, 1992, pp. 184–202
Grose, Francis, *A Classical Dictionary of the Vulgar Tongue*. Second, corrected and enlarged edition. London, 1788
Hart, George, *The Routledge Dictionary of Egyptian Gods and Goddesses*. London and New York, 2005
Henderson, George, *Survivals in Beliefs Among the Celts*. James Maclehose and Sons, Glasgow, 1911
Henderson, William, *Folklore from the Northern Counties of England and the Borders*. The Folk-lore Society, London, 1879
Hulme, F E, *Natural History Lore and Legend*. Bernard Quaritch, London, 1895
In-Sŏb, Zŏng , *Folk Tales from Korea*. Routledge & Kegan Paul, London, 1952
Jessop, Violet, *Titanic Survivor*. Sheridan House, New York, 1997
Lang, Andrew, *The Brown Fairy Book*. Longmans, Green and Co., London, 1904
Lang, Andrew, *The Crimson Fairy Book*. Longmans, Green and Co., London, 1935
Lange-Athinodorou, Eva, Bubastis City of the Feline Goddess, Golden House Publications, 2024
Macleod Banks, Mary, *British Calendar Customs, Orkney and Shetland*. The Folk-lore Society, London, 1946
Magnússon, Eiríkr and Powell, George E J (trans), *Icelandic Legends* (Collected by Jón Árnason). Longmans, Green and Co., London, 1866
Málek, Jaromír, *The Cat in Ancient Egypt*. British Museum Press, London, 1993
Massignon, Geneviève, *Folktales of France*. University of Chicago Press, Chicago, 1968
Mertvago, Peter (ed), *Dictionary of 1,000 Russian Proverbs*. Hippocrene Books, New York, 1998
Mitford, A B, *Tales of Old Japan*. Macmillan, London, 1883
Moiser, Chris, Mystery Big Cats of Dorset, Inspiring Places Publishing, Hampshire, 2007
Monger, George. 'Dragons and Big Cats.' Folklore, vol. 103, no. 2,

1992, pp. 203–06
Opie, Iona and Tatem, Moira (ed), *A Dictionary of Superstitions.* Oxford University Press, Oxford, 1989
O'Sullivan, Sean (ed), *Folktales of Ireland.* University of Chicago Press, Chicago and London, 1966
Pinch, Geraldine, *Handbook of Egyptian Mythology.* ABC-CLIO, Santa Barbara, 2002
Ransome, Arthur, *Old Peter's Russian Tales.* Thomas Nelson and Sons, London, 1935
Serpell, James A (8 June 2000), 'Domestication and History of the Cat'. In Dennis C Turner and Patrick Bateson (eds), *The Domestic Cat: the Biology of its Behaviour*, pp.177–192 Cambridge University Press, Cambridge, 1988
Sommer, H Oskar, *The Vulgate Version of the Arthurian Romances.* Volume I. Carnegie Institution of Washington, Washington, 1908
Sommer, H Oskar, *The Vulgate Version of the Arthurian Romances.* Volume II. Carnegie Institution of Washington, Washington, 1908
Steiner, Roland, 'Superstitions and Beliefs from Central Georgia', The Journal of American Folklore, Oct-Dec, 1899, Vol 12, No.47, 1899, pp.261-271
Stewart, W Grant, *Popular Superstitions of the Highlanders of Scotland.* Archibald Constable and Company, London, 1823
Summers, Montague, *The Vampire, His Kith and Kin.* Kegan Paul, Trench, Trubner & Co., London, 1928
Topsell, Edward, *Historie of Four-footed Beasts.* William Jaggard, London, 1607
Trevelyan, Mary, *Folk-Lore and Folk-Stories of Wales.* Elliot Stock, London, 1909
Udal, John Symonds, *Dorsetshire Folk-Lore.* Dorset Books, 1989
Vocelle, L A, *Revered and Reviled: A Complete History of the Domestic Cat.* Great Cat Publications, 2017
Winsham, Willow, *Accused: British Witches Throughout History.* Pen & Sword Books, Barnsley, 2022
Young, Peter, 'Origins of the Cheshire Cat'. *Cheshire History*, Number 55 (2015–2016), pp.184–193

INDEX